THINKING ABOUT DRAWING

THINKING ABOUT DRAWING

An Introduction to Themes and Concepts

SIMON GRENNAN

BLOOMSBURY VISUAL ARTS

LONDON · NEW YORK · OXFORD · NEW DELHI · SYDNEY

BLOOMSBURY VISUAL ARTS
Bloomsbury Publishing Plc
50 Bedford Square, London, WC1B 3DP, UK
1385 Broadway, New York, NY 10018, USA
29 Earlsfort Terrace, Dublin 2, Ireland

BLOOMSBURY, BLOOMSBURY VISUAL ARTS and the
Diana logo are trademarks of Bloomsbury Publishing Plc

First published in Great Britain 2022

Cover design: Louise Dugdale
Cover image © Hand drawing by Undefined Undefined / Getty images

A catalogue record for this book is available from the British Library.

A catalog record for this book is available from the Library of Congress.

ISBN: HB: 978-1-3502-6943-9
          PB: 978-1-3502-6593-6
          ePDF: 978-1-3502-6595-0
          eBook: 978-1-3502-6594-3

Typeset by Integra Software Services Pvt. Ltd.
Printed and bound in India

To find out more about our authors and books visit www.bloomsbury.com
and sign up for our newsletters.

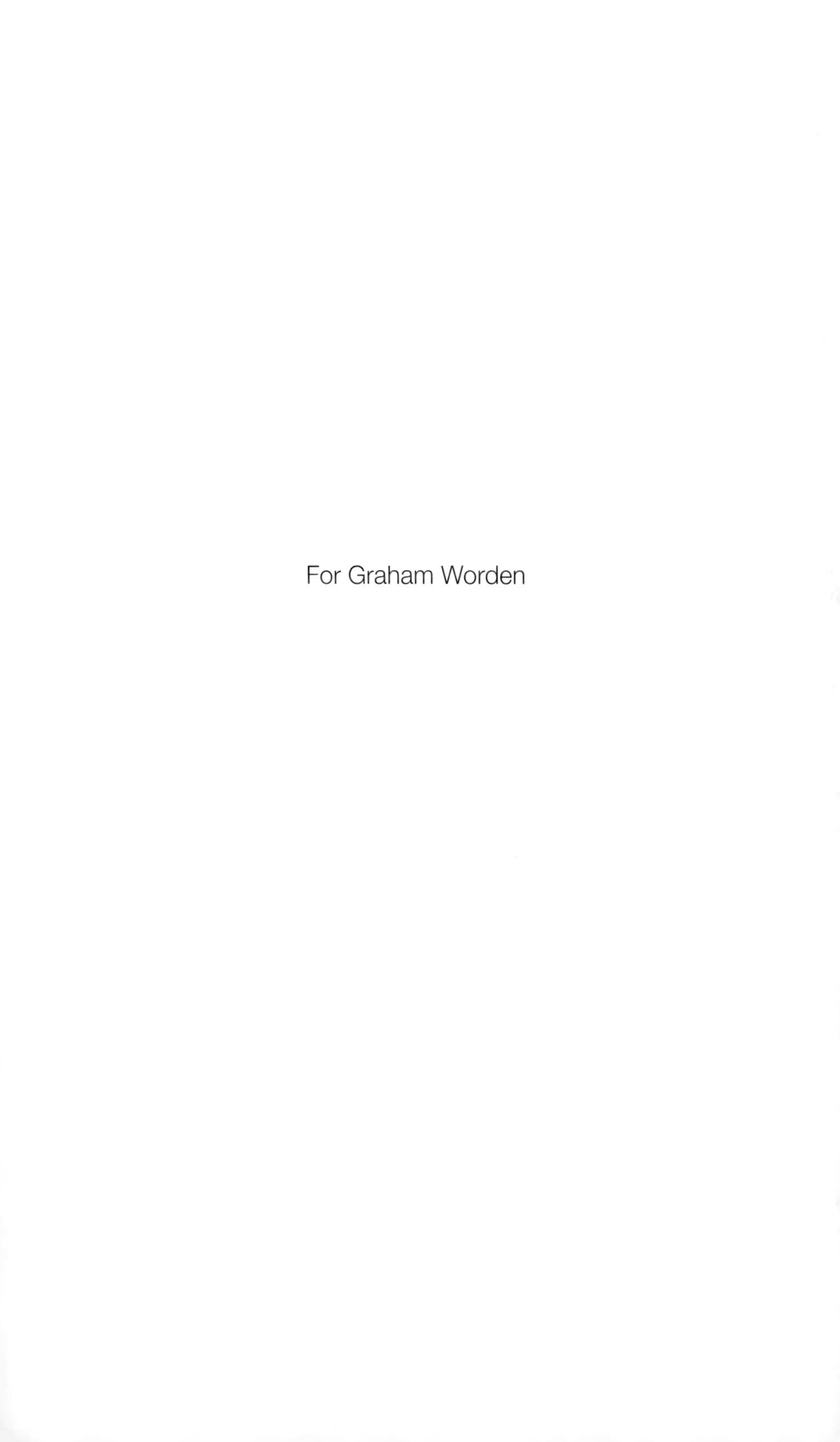

For Graham Worden

CONTENTS

ILLUSTRATIONS

INTRODUCTION: WHAT IS DRAWING?

Speaking in 2020, the celebrated illustrator Quentin Blake described how he draws his characters:

> Part of you is doing this identifying with the person, being that person. The other bit of your mind is thinking, 'Is this in the right place on the page?'

Blake's description provides a neat summary of what is involved in drawing. We understand his aims in making a drawing and how he is drawing. These two things also give us an idea about the situation in which he is drawing. He is drawing a scene and wants to understand the characters involved in it, so that a viewer will also understand them, by looking at what he has drawn. To do this, Blake visually interrogates the scene (even if the scene is imaginary), and his scrutiny guides his placement of **marks** on the page. His body manipulates the media he has chosen and enables the marks. And there's the drawing.

> **MARK** A mark is any visual item that reproduces and represents the functional aspects of the system of representation from which it gains its meaning. These systems of representation include writing, mapping, any spatial projection, depictions and, ultimately, the conditions of the situation in which a mark is made and seen. In the sense that mark making defines drawing, the drawn mark cannot be identified outside a system of representation because it is the system that gives a mark meaning. This is what distinguishes drawn marks from any other random mark that we might see. No specific technology or set of social circumstances ever defines the mark.

For millennia drawing has been conceived as an exploratory activity, mediating between the vision of the **drafter** and the **object** of their drawing, in order to reveal hidden relationships, to direct attention, to scrutinize the material world and to provide plans for further action.

> **DRAFTER** A drafter makes drawings.

> **OBJECT** An object is something observed. This definition relies upon the idea that human consciousness is subjective, that the world is not simply experienced when it is observed but, rather, the world is produced by observation. The human subject observes and the object is the thing (or the world) observed.

These ways of thinking about drawing underwent a dramatic transformation in the twentieth century, particularly in Western traditions of visual culture. In part, the idea that drawing interrogates and arranges the object in view, preparing the way for subsequent, more significant activities (such as constructing a machine, building a house or painting a portrait), was thought to promote outdated status relationships that the century sought to overturn, such as the relationship between the blueprint and the house, or the sketch and the painting.

With increasing globalization, drawing traditions have also become increasingly visible and comprehensible to drafters in other traditions. As a result, many key ideas about drawing, as well as techniques, materials and reasons for making drawings, are shared by widely different people and applied in widely different contexts. The idea that Western traditions have a monopoly upon, or even a leading claim to, ideas about drawing has always been inaccurate, short sighted or prejudiced. Since the twentieth century, it has been increasingly easy for drafters to see, understand and apply ideas about drawing that derive from other people, other places and other times.

At the same time, the long history of drawing has suggested that it might be an archetypal human activity, apparently beyond the restraining conventions of any particular society or time. The comparative directness of the **technical** aspects of drawing has also attested to its status as a **medium** of psychological truth. Drawing is very old indeed. Its simplicity and directness appear to offer an authentic glimpse of a drafter's mind.

TECHNOLOGY Technology is any item or situation that modifies, transforms or produces capacities of the human body.

MEDIUM A medium is a set of agreed circumstances in which information is stored and transmitted. These agreed circumstances are often tied to specific forms of representation, which are themselves often tied to specific materials and social situations. For example, the medium of writing produces all of the wide range of circumstances in which writing is used, whilst the drawing medium produces all of the wide range of circumstances in which drawing is used. The circumstances in which a medium is used and the forms it adopts can be extremely various.

More recently, these ideas have been expanded, contradicted and revised in a current renaissance in drawing activities, encompassing a wide range of motives and explanations, as well as a new raft of technical processes. Drawing is now considered to be both plan and product, to be both mind map and body trace, **digital** and **analogue**, in a wide range of contexts that examine society and the human **subject**, as well as representing and producing them.

DIGITAL Digital is a method of generating representations by re-coding the things that are represented as series of two numerical values, 'zero' or 'one'. This code accumulates in different sequences to create commands. It is these commands that generate representations in different media.

ANALOGUE Analogue media directly reproduces and rearranges properties that it shares with the objects it represents. This direct reproduction and rearrangement is described as analogous. For example, the colour of an analogue mark might be the same as the colour of the object it represents. A yellow mark might indicate a banana or a shaft of yellow sunlight because all of these things share the property 'yellow'.

SUBJECT The subject is a human observer of the world. This definition relies upon the idea that human consciousness is subjective, that the world is not simply experienced when it is observed but, rather, the world is produced by observation. The human subject observes and the object is the thing (or the world) observed.

Under these conditions, more than ever, a fundamental question remains: what is drawing?

To those who either disregard or advocate drawing, definitions of drawing are often self-evident. They associate the medium with one or other of its many iterations, rather than taking a view on the medium as a whole. They make judgements according to the particular characteristics, opportunities and inhibitions presented by one situation alone – usually the situation in which they find themselves. Sometimes, association with an exclusive social hierarchy or an historic tradition defines drawing. For example, the European traditions of studio fine art retain a high social status, exemplified by the Royal Drawing School, London. The millennia-old traditions of Chinese calligraphy are still maintained by the contemporary Xizhi School of Calligraphy and Painting. However, neither the circumstances nor the traditions of either fine art studio practice or calligraphy offer a complete definition of drawing.

Everyday, popular distinctions also hinder rather than help the definition of drawing. In particular, popular ideas of the role of the human hand in drawing continue to be confused with some of the issues raised by the different media that drafters use – and not only with the advent of digital technology. This insistence, on the significance of the human hand, is rooted in some very long-standing ideas about the importance of the residual **trace** of an individual body for drawing, representing an individual mind. This idea is reflected in the special status frequently granted to children's drawings. Drawings made by untrained children are often thought to represent unmediated emotions or to be representations of an authentic world view.

> **TRACE** Traces are the direct remnants of drawing activities. Traces index, or point to, the activity of the body from which they originate, but they also leave remnants. Trace is a subset of index.

On the other hand, the mechanical products of drafting, representing the design of products or of digital images, are often not considered to be drawings at all. This idea follows the fact that they are produced with the aid of machines. According to these popular rationales, the direct presence of the drafter's body is itself a definition of drawing.

Yet drawings have been made in too many contradictory ways and in too wide a range of circumstances, to be readily defined by one situation or another, or by a too-dogmatic insistence on the presence of a drafter's hand.

Confusions and contradictions abound. For example, drawing can also appear to be an activity defined by rules, such as those determining the location of a mark on a surface in a perspective or three-dimensional **spatial projection system**. It is also thought of as direct, unconstrained and hence emotionally expressive. Drawing has been identified with the

> **SPATIAL PROJECTION SYSTEM** A spatial projection system is a closed system of visual representation in which the location of marks on a two-dimensional surface systematically corresponds to the relative proximities between three-dimensional coordinates found in the viewed scene that is being represented. Spatial projection systems always create a systematic equivalence of the location of two-dimensional marks and three-dimensional coordinates.

visual imitation of the visible world, from the earliest of times. But the act of drawing often also ignores this relationship and encompasses all types of writing and schematic planning, doodling, decorative pattern making and tracing.

Drawing has a long history of being explained as a spatial art rather than a temporal art (that is, representing space rather than time). However, this is contradicted by another long-lived idea – the idea of the material presence of drawing. The material presence of the drawing is rooted in the movement of the drafter's body when the drawing is made. These movements of the drafter's body underpin many of the specific sequences of actions that have shaped themselves into the craft traditions of drawing. In addition, the historic and social circumstances in which drawings are made are even more various than the technology used in their production, or the ideas that give drawings significance.

The variety above is enough to suggest that definitions of drawing have been both subsumed by technology and have superseded it, that definitions have been both determined by the body and are independent of it and that they have been by-words both for visual mimicry and illusion and for every other type of mark.

One way of bundling together such a variety of situations, ideas and actions is to propose that all drawings share some characteristics, or that all drawing activities share some functions. Some theorists of drawing have tried to identify these. An immediate shortcoming of the proposal that all drawings share things lies in the fact that definitions are always the products of their time. Despite often seeming to define the world in which they appear, definitions are grounded in the circumstances in which they are made. We can talk easily of a drawing as an object, but less easily about the possibilities and impossibilities of the circumstances in which it was made. For example, if we think of the drawn design of a British eighteenth-century terraced house, we do not think so easily of the essential circumstances under which the design was thought up and the house built, such as the increased availability of fresh food in the centre of cities in the period. However, the drawn design and the circumstances were intimately co-dependent.

When we think that drawing is only defined by the physical **properties** of drawings, we mistakenly objectify drawing and set it apart from the world. The surfaces of drawings can appear to dazzle the viewer to such an extent that drawing's materials, intentions and uses are obscured. Historically, this process, along with the idea of the personal, expressive potential of drawings, has done much to distort our view of drawing.

PROPERTIES Properties are experiences attributed to things. For example, the property 'red' might be attributed to an apple. Redness is not definitive of all apples, so redness exemplifies a particular (red) apple, without permanently modifying our expectations of apples in general. Words often substituted for 'properties' include 'features', 'characteristics' or 'qualities'.

A series of topics emerge from ideas about drawings and drawing activities that are dependent for significance on the circumstances in which they appear. These can be summarized as **imitation**, **mark**, **trace** and **story**. The chapters in this book consider these related topics in turn.

Chapter 1, *Imitation*, introduces one of the oldest and most influential ideas about drawing, which proposes that its purpose is to create visual imitations of the visible world. The chapter explains the relationship between this idea and visual illusion. An ideal visual illusion makes invisible the medium in which it is made. The chapter describes how this ideal suppression of drawing media, in favour of the representation of scenes, has gone hand in hand with two further very old ideas: the idea that visual images are motionless and the related idea that visual images cannot show **stories**.

STORY Story encompasses everything that is told or shown, as structurally and functionally distinct from the activities of telling or showing. This definition allows the widest range of representations to be considered as stories, in every medium. It contradicts older definitions, which insist that stories can only be told in verbal media.

Chapter 2, Mark, explores the significance of different media for creating visual imitations. It introduces the idea of visual **depiction** (that is, seeing the way in which a visual image is made, whilst also visualizing the scene that it represents). It considers the ways in which definitions of drawing came to encompass mark making in different media, for different purposes. The chapter describes the long-standing association of drawing with planning and notation, with the **visualization** of thought processes, the visualization of non-visual systems (such as the visualization in writing of non-visual language systems) and the emergence of the dominant idea of the **line**.

DEPICTION Depiction is a type of visual representation defined by both seeing the materials with which the depiction is made whilst simultaneously imagining that we see the object of the depiction. In depictions, the dual experience of vision (seeing marks) and visualization ('seeing-in' the object of depiction) is unlike any other experience of visual representation. In everyday language, the word 'figurative' is often substituted for 'depictive'.

VISUALIZATION Visualization is visual imagining, a type of mental representation. Whilst not necessarily related to experiences of the world outside the body, such as vision, visualizations are themselves perceived. As such, visualizations conform in structure and function to perceptions, even if they are not related to any other perceived experience.

LINE First, line is an abstract idea, representing two dimensions, extending the idea of a one-dimensional point. Neither point nor line has any material manifestation. They are ideas. A point is the idea of a location in space and a line is the idea of either an accumulation of adjacent points or the distance between two remote points. Second, however, line is also a trace of the direction in which a drafter forces the drawing medium, the material making a mark.

Chapter 3, Trace, outlines how definitions of drawing have been derived from the capacities of different media and the technical traditions of different crafts. It explores the transformation of this idea after the Second World War, when drawing was increasingly defined according to the capacities of the drafter's body rather than the capacities of different media. The chapter notes that ideas of the drafter's body were implicit in much older ideas about drawing. In particular, it considers the relationships between the drafter's body and the concept of individual drawing **style**. The chapter then looks in detail at the idea of the trace of the drafter's body, which is currently central to thinking about drawing, explaining how this trace points to the presence of the body, as a direct remnant of mark making.

STYLE Style is the specific degrees to which the manufacture of an individual representation or object resembles or differs from the manufacture of other manufactured representations or objects.

Chapter 4, Story, continues the exploration of current ideas about how drawing traces the drafter's body. It brings together gesture, movement, the drawn mark and, in depictive drawings, the represented scene. The chapter examines how drawings are currently understood as existing in time and as showing time. It introduces concepts about the representation of time in drawings – first, the idea that the representations that drawings show must have a past and a future, although these are not shown; second, the idea that drawn marks always record the duration of their own making; and third, the idea that the time taken to make a drawing is quite distinct from the time that the drawing represents. These ideas cross long-established boundaries between ideas about the visual and performing arts and ideas about language, speech and writing. The chapter concludes with an exploration of current ideas about drawn stories, including the recasting of the drafter as a visual narrator.

Chapter 5, Drawing today, brings these diverse, historical and current strands together. It considers the challenges and opportunities facing contemporary drawing. It stands back from the previous topics that define drawing: imitation, mark, trace and story. The chapter asks how the different circumstances in which drawings are made influence the drafter's **feelings** about making drawings. It evaluates creative responses that contemporary drafters are making to developments in digital media. It maps these onto the older traditions of thinking about the significance of media for drawing and the current central place of the body in defining the wide variety of types of contemporary drawing. The chapter concludes with an overview of some of the newest emerging approaches to drawing, forging new and revised categorizations of time, story showing, virtual embodiment, mark making and visual imitation.

FEELING Feeling is often thought of as spontaneous emotion and sensation. However, feeling also encompasses some types of judgement that are not simply accompanied by spontaneously occurring emotions or sensations. These include ethical judgements of right and wrong, about which is commonly said 'I don't feel right about' a situation or 'it feels wrong'.

1

IMITATION

The idea that drawing can be described and assessed as a visual imitation of the visible world is one of the oldest ways of thinking about drawing. It derives from the philosopher Plato (429?–347 BCE), in the classical period of ancient Greece (Illustration 1.1). In a comparison of the visual and verbal arts, Plato claimed that the function of visual images is '**mimesis**', that is, to imitate the visible world. This idea, of mimesis, appears to be simple, because it predates current distinctions that we might make between the different techniques and media used to make visual images, such as drawing and painting. If Plato's idea is to be understood, these technical differences really need to be set aside. For Plato, current categories of drawing and painting were not meaningful, because they did not exist in the fourth century BCE.

MIMESIS The visual imitation of the visible world.

What is most significant (and influential) about Plato's idea of imitation is his conception of visual images as motionless. He thought that visual images cannot represent change and also thought that the processes by which these images are made are absolutely insignificant. According to him, there is no meaning to be found in the work of the drafter until the visual image reaches the point of imitating the visible world.

Plato contrasted this idea with a definition of poetry, in which the activity of verbally telling a story is paramount rather than the idea of achieving an imitation that aims to become a visual illusion. For Plato, poetry was an art that could represent change because it involved description and action, whereas drawings could not as they always remain still. The residue of this idea survives, against the odds. As recently as 2001, art historian Eileen Adams (b.1962) was able to claim

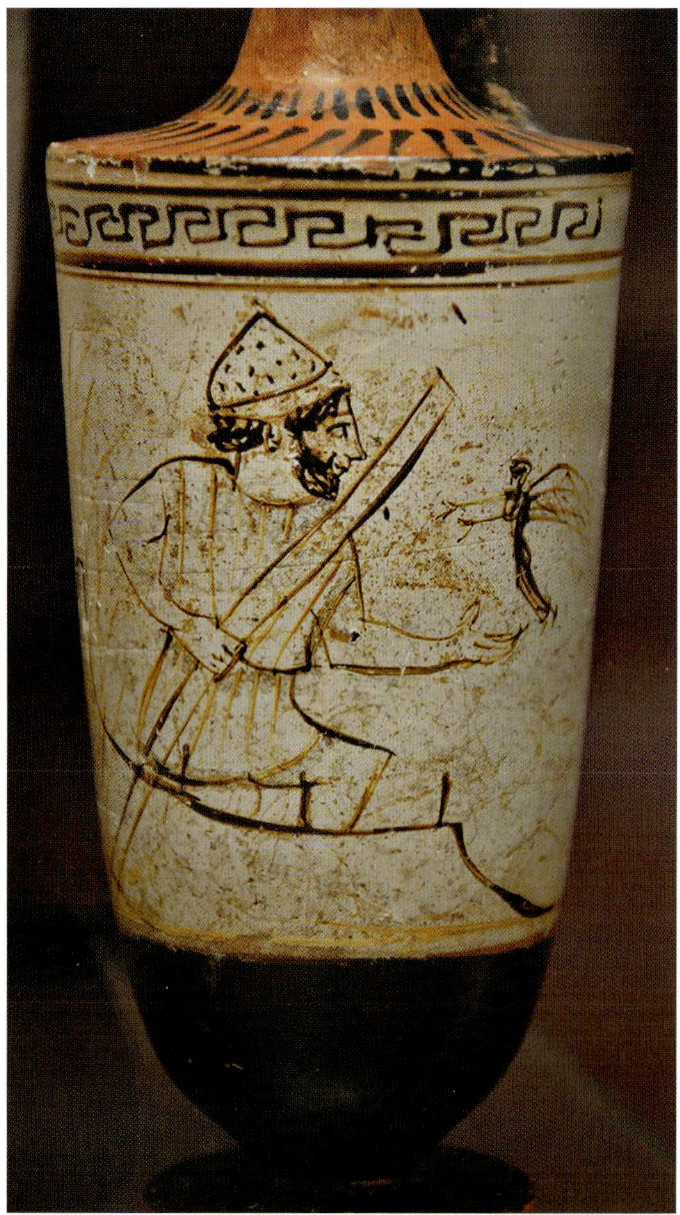

ILLUSTRATION 1.1 The Tymbos Painter (attributed), *Attic Red Figure (White Ground) Lekythos with Charon* (detail), 500–450 BCE. Ashmolean Museum, Oxford, by Following Hadrian. Licensed under CC BY-SA 2.0.

that the value of drawing activities reside in their scrutiny and imitation of the visible world, as well as their interpretation and notation.

However, despite the considerable influence of this residual idea, we can immediately see difficulties with the idea of visual imitation. In fact, these difficulties arise from the technology used to make visual images. Plato is silent about the degree to which an image should imitate the visible world. He does not consider the point at which an image achieves imitation. A perfect visual imitation is an illusion, rationally speaking, in which the viewer is not aware of the technology used in the production of the image but rather perceives the representation as the object that it represents, as a view of the real thing. Experiences of true visual illusions are the stock-in-trade of entertainers such as stage magicians (Illustration 1.2). The type of situation in which a viewer actually takes an image for the object it represents is so unusual that it points to the

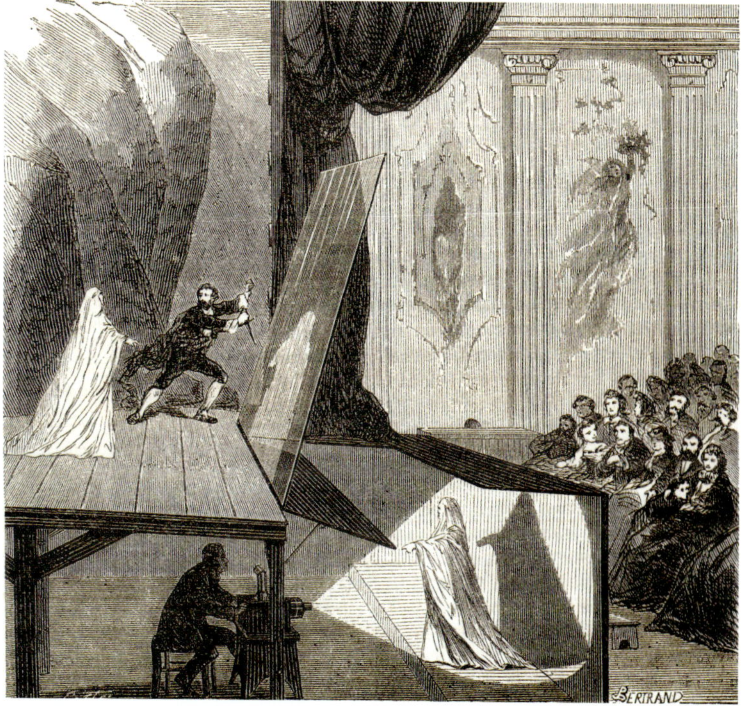

ILLUSTRATION 1.2 Bertrand 'Pepper's Ghost', *Le Monde Illustré*, engraving, 1862.

fact that either literal imitation was not what Plato meant or Plato had misconceived the function of visual images.

These considerably influential, residual ideas have not escaped subsequent commentators, but the overriding idea of the stillness of visual images remained largely unexamined. This was until the advent of lens-based visual media in the nineteenth century (such as photography) and the growth of ideas about storytelling in the twentieth and twenty-first centuries.

The role of different techniques in producing visual imitations is a long-standing topic, of which Platonic conceptions of the different status of drawing, painting and plan making are the outdated survivors. How does the material used to produce a mimetic image influence the way in which the image is understood? Is there more or less emotional potential in paint, ink, pencil or pixel, or in scratching, rubbing, splashing or computer programming?

The threshold of visualization and the problem of media

The contradiction between visible imitation and the means by which the image is drawn is exemplified best in drawings that self-consciously seek to test this contradiction. What are the limits beyond which the imagined scenes shown in depictions begin to fragment, simply becoming views of the materials used to make them? This is a boundary of imagination across which the viewer spontaneously travels when they see a depiction. This might be difficult to understand. When the viewer looks at drawn marks on a surface, the mind of the viewer imagines that the viewer is experiencing their own experience of seeing the drawn scene. They imagine that they are experiencing themselves seeing a scene, when they look at drawn marks on a surface.

Viewers themselves establish this boundary between material and scene, and it is different for every viewer. Either they visualize a depicted scene at the same time as they see the marked surface, they experience indeterminacy (as they struggle to visualize the scene) or they only see the marked surface and cannot visualize the scene.

The art of producing this moment has a long history, associated with a very wide range of ideas. On the one hand, the fifteenth-century Chinese drawing traditions of 'haboku' (broken ink) and 'hatsuboku' (splashed ink) aimed to produce this visual indeterminacy, so as to promote and represent a Chan Buddhist religious idea of the similarity of spiritual transcendence and experiences of daily life. The moment of indeterminacy can be prolonged indefinitely (Illustration 1.3).

On the other hand, Alexander Cozens's (1717–1786) manual of drawing *A New Method of Assisting the Invention in Drawing Original Compositions of Landscape* (1786), laid out a method of blotting paper with ink so as to produce shapes that prompted students to imagine scenes. Cozens had been using this method since the 1750s to teach drawing students how to liberate their visual imaginations, by struggling to make visual imitations of scenes from random marks on a page (Illustration 1.4).

Of particular historic significance, for thinking about the relationship between the drawn mark and visual imitation, was a sixteenth-century Italian public relations campaign, which was undertaken to promote the value of the work of the painter Titian (Tiziano Vicelli, 1490–1576) by his friend the poet Pietro Aretino (1492–1556). Aretino launched the idea that there is a distinction between line and **colour**, bundled with the idea that the use of colour allows visual imitations of things that the use of drawn lines does not. The idea arose in discussions making 'paragone' or 'comparisons' between the different depictive potential of drawings and paintings. On the one hand, the Italian word 'colore' meant the depiction of the 'air', or the light and atmosphere of a scene, while 'colorito' meant the technical methods for producing a depiction of this light and atmosphere. 'Colorito' techniques were defined by

COLOUR Colour is the wavelength of light reflected from objects, resulting in perceived and imagined associations between these wavelengths and other material properties. Although these wavelengths are themselves properties, they are always perceived according to different biological capacities in different creatures, including humans.

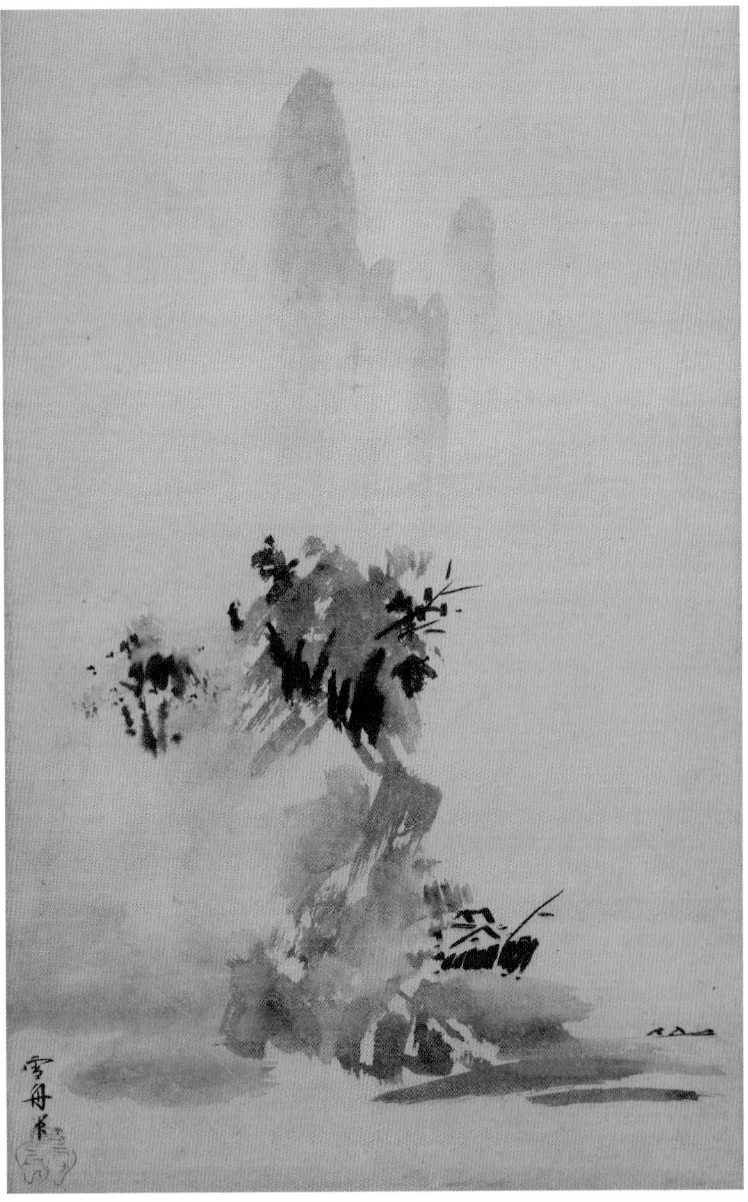

ILLUSTRATION 1.3 Sesshu Toyo, *Haboku-Sansui,* ink on paper, 1495.

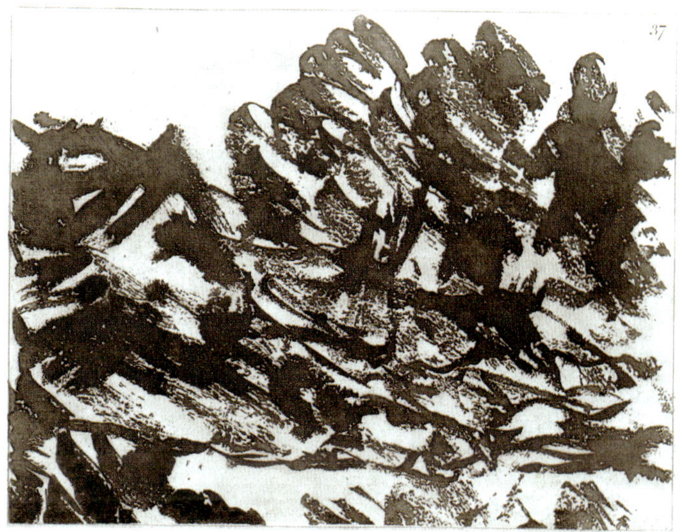

ILLUSTRATION 1.4 Alexander Cozens, *A New Method of Assisting the Invention in Drawing Original Compositions of Landscape*, ink on paper, 1786.

blending lighter and darker **tones** and blending different colours. On the other hand, the Italian word 'disegno' meant the identification of divisions and contours, or drawn lines, as a method for depicting silhouettes, encompassed volumes and the boundaries between one object and another.

TONE Tone is a relative degree of the presence of light (lightness or darkness), measured by comparison with other degrees of light.

This Venetian discussion of 'colore' and 'disegno' was not intended to create a new distinction between media. It was intended to promote Titian's technique of blending colours. Titian blended colours in order to represent the 'air' or the atmosphere in which his scenes appeared, rather than outlining the objects and characters of which they were comprised.

Historically, however, Aretino achieved just such a distinction between different media. At the same time, he established visual depiction as a distinct category of visual experience, defined by both seeing the materials that produce the representation whilst also visualizing the represented scene. Ideally, before Aretino, those materials that made a visual imitation were invisible. In drawing traditions in the West, he established that both materials and representation were important parts of the visual image. Aretino recognized that the material used to make the image and the artist's technique of using those materials, were not ideally invisible or insignificant, as Plato proposed. Rather, the way in which the image is made and the scene that the image represents mutually affect each other.

Depiction and visualization

In the twentieth century, the experience of seeing both the materials and the represented object at the same time has become known as visual depiction. Although we might use the word to describe a range of types of visual representation, it now also has a specific meaning. Depiction is a unique type of visual representation, described most memorably by philosopher Richard Wollheim (1923–2003) as 'seeing-in'. It always involves seeing the materials that the depiction is made out of, whilst also visualizing the scene that the depiction shows.

Visualization, that is, visual imagining, is a type of mental representation. You don't have to see something to imagine that you are seeing it. You do perceive that you are seeing something (even though it is imaginary), in the same way as you might actually see something. Although the metaphor for visualization – the 'mind's eye' – remains strong, visualizations are not actually images but mental processes. These mental processes closely follow the mental processes of experiences of vision themselves.

Experiencing depiction involves imagining that you see yourself seeing a scene. It differs from both vision and visualization (or straightforward visual imagining) because it always involves this experience of seeing the drawing and visualizing the absent object at the same time. Hence, the experience of depiction has a definitive structure, which distinguishes it from the structure of other types of visual representation and is a unique phenomenon. The experience of seeing marks while at the same time experiencing visualization is unlike any other experience of visual representation.

Many ideas about drawing derive from consideration of this combined experience. First, the colour pencil drawing *Gold Seal* by SirSlasher (n.d.) exemplifies drawing as a visual imitation of the visible world and proposes that drawings show still scenes and are **objective**. The drawing shares visual properties with a colour photograph. The individual drawn marks are not visible. Rather, they are subsumed in tonal contrasts that mimic the chemical or digital effects of light on a light-sensitive photographic surface (Illustration 1.5).

> **OBJECTIVE (adjective)** A description of a set of circumstances made without the use of judgement. An objective description aims to establish impartiality, or an absence of judgement, by identifying properties or characteristics that are self-evidencing. As such, objectivity (the capacity to make objective descriptions) is often associated with quantification and measurement, as distinct from emotion or sensation.

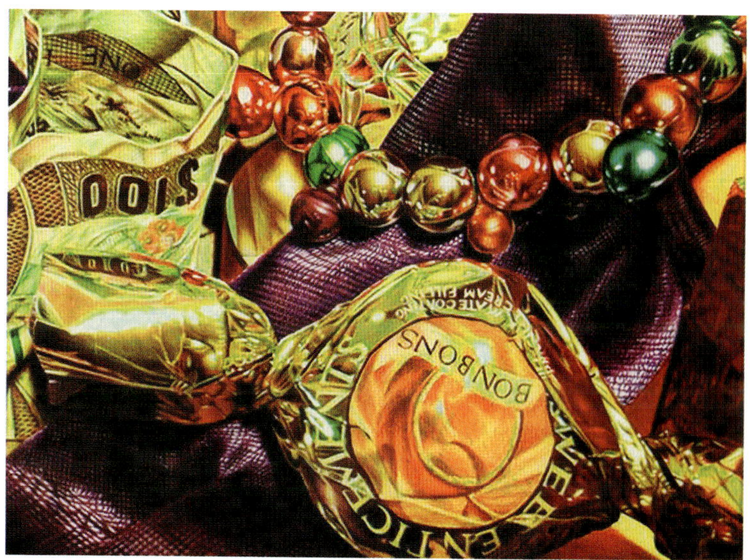

ILLUSTRATION 1.5 SirSlasher, *Gold Seal*, pencil, 2011. Licensed under CC BY 2.0.

Second, the idea of the significance of the materials with which a drawing is made generates ideas of the significance of the mark, its source in bodily activity and environment and, hence, concepts of motion, **subjectivity** and story. Depictive drawings in which materials have significance bring together the imagined world of the drawn image and the physical and social world of the drafter. An eighteenth-century miniature drawing by an unknown Rajasthani artist provides an example of these worlds being brought together (Illustration 1.6). The real gold applied to the drawing literally shares the properties of the depicted gold of the furniture and fabrics. The applied gold also represents the properties of the depicted golden light touching the clouds behind the tent.

> **SUBJECTIVE** A description of a set of circumstances made using judgement. A subjective description establishes a partial view based on the human subject's emotions and ideas. As such, subjectivity (the capacity to make judgements) produces the identity of the subject or produces the relationships between the subject and the world rather than describing observations of the world.

The work of Mexican artist Jerónimo López Ramírez, known as Dr Lakra (b.1972), provides another example. The most significant thing about his drawing *Sin título / Untitled (Hiroshima Tomonohira Take-Emon)* is that it has been made on top of an older woodblock print of a sumo wrestler, of the type exemplified by the Japanese artist Kunisada Utagawa (1786–1865). It brings together the physical and social world of Dr Lakra, in the twenty-first century and the nineteenth-century world depicted in the print. Dr Lakra is a tattooist. In this drawing, he has both depicted a nineteenth-century sumo wrestler with tattoos and tattooed a nineteenth-century drawing (Illustrations 1.7 and 1.8).

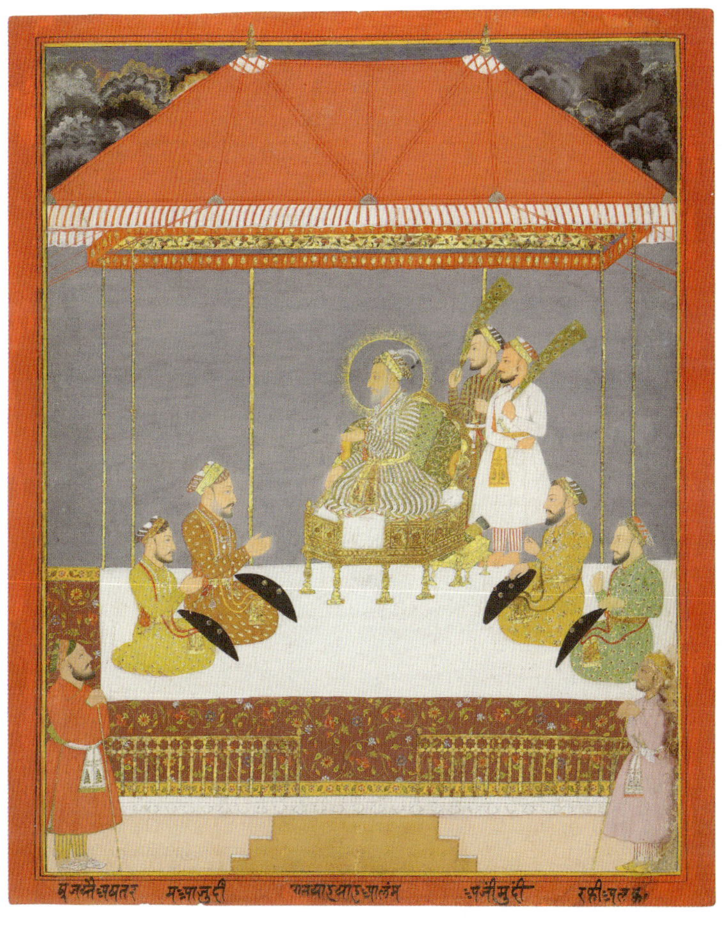

ILLUSTRATION 1.6 Anonymous, *Emperor Bahadur Shah I, seated on a throne, with his son*, paint and gold on paper, 1710.

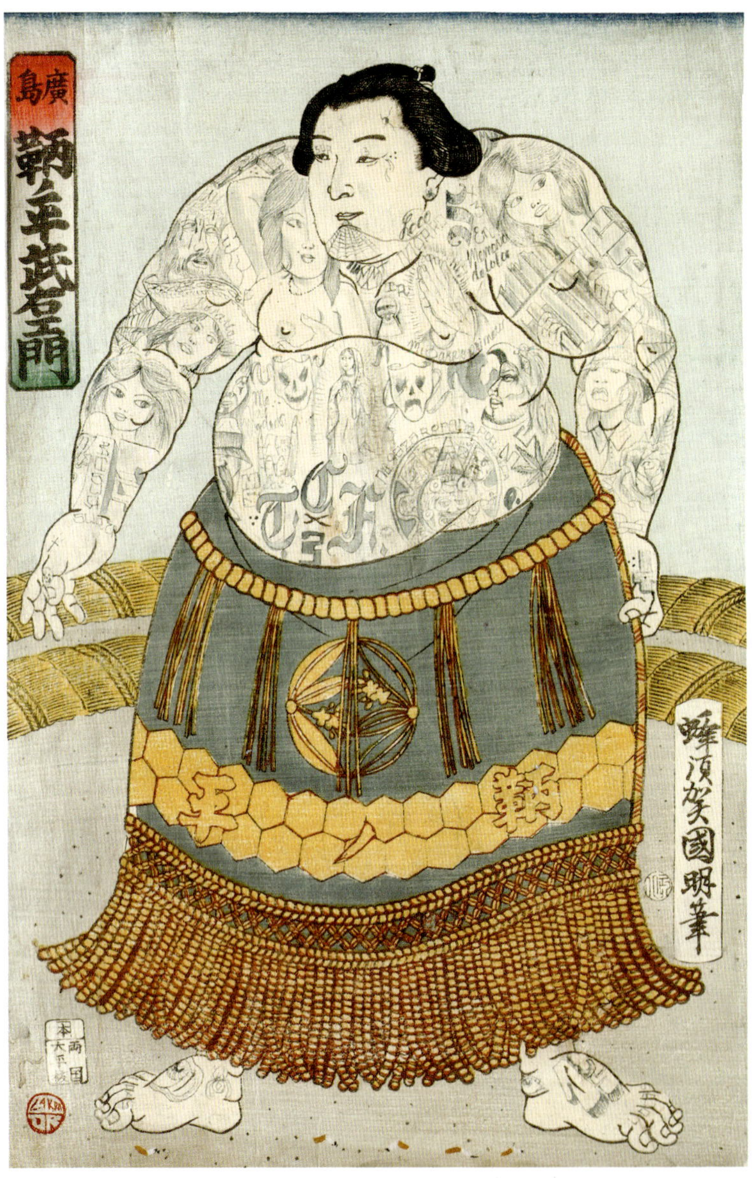

ILLUSTRATION 1.7 Dr Lakra, *Sin título / Untitled (Hiroshima Tomonohira Take-Emon)*, ink on woodblock print, 2007. Courtesy of the artist and Kurimanzutto, Mexico City / New York. Photograph Estudio Michel Zabé.

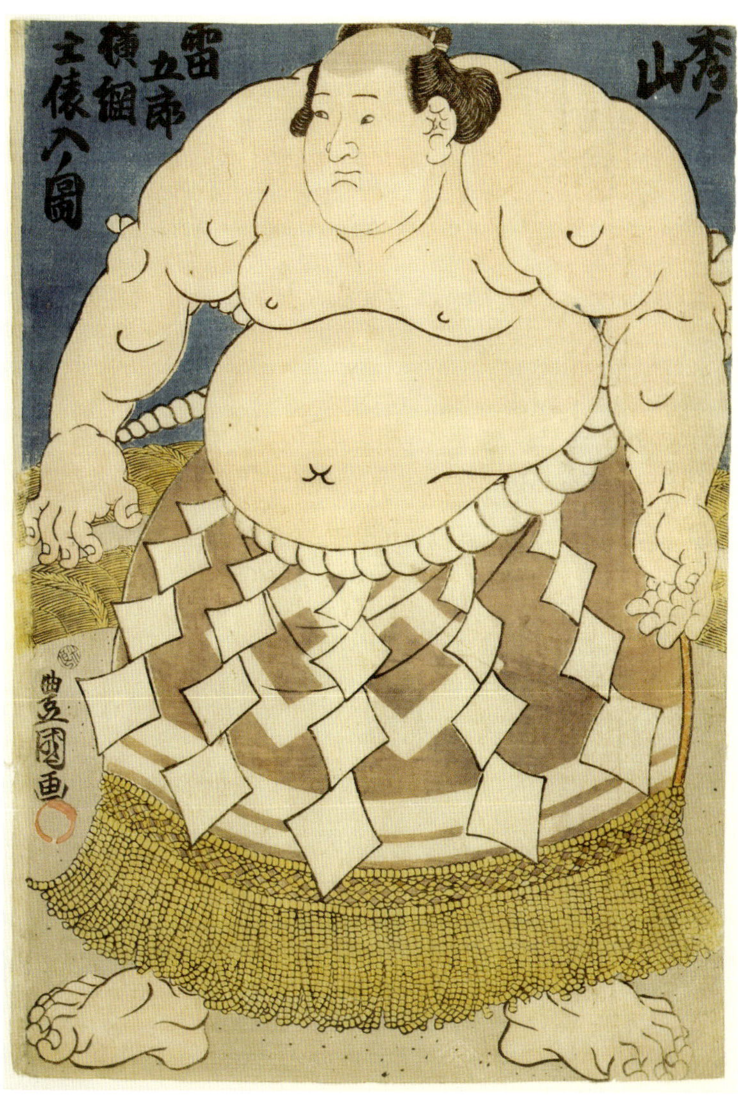

ILLUSTRATION 1.8 Kunisada Utagawa *Hidenoyama*, woodblock print, 1845.

Imitating vision and imitating drawing

Rather than being contradicted by the attention paid to the moving body, it turns out that vision remains a strong focus for discussions about drawing. Concepts of vision bring together sight, perception, visual imagination and engagement – in other words, the ways in which drafters make use of technical resources to produce media and make use of ideas, to determine the significance of different media. For example, the random marks created on a leather jacket through wear can be seen as visual records of the jacket's history. The marks provide visible evidence for the idea that the jacket has been worn (Illustration 1.9). The fashion and fabric design industry practice of adding fabric swatches to concept drawings also provides visible evidence, in different media, for the concept of the design (Illustration 1.10).

The philosopher John Berger (1926–2017) claimed that the task of observing and making use of drawing, to scrutinize and understand what is visible, is essential to the other types of drawing activities concerned with ideas and memory. He described three types of drawing activity: (a) those undertaken in order to scrutinize the visible world (which he calls 'observational'), (b) those undertaken to present or demonstrate an idea and (c) those undertaken by recalling memories. His description falls firmly into the tradition of thinking about drawing as imitation, even though ideas do not need to resemble anything visible.

Of course, this attempt to root drawing in scrutiny of the visible world hides within it a simple contradiction between objectivity and subjectivity. For Berger, observational drawing (which aspires to be an objective imitation of what is seen) also relies on the visual memory of the drafter because what the drafter sees is always adjudicated by what the drafter knows. In Berger's sense, even an observational drawing 'from life' is never strictly objective because the drafter makes use of knowledge as well as vision to make the drawing. Drawings made by eyewitnesses to events display this tendency well, such as Amos Bad Heart Bull's drawings of the *Battle of Little Bighorn*, which he made many years after the event. He drew what he recalled having seen but also what he knew about those parts of the battle that he did not see (Illustration 1.11).

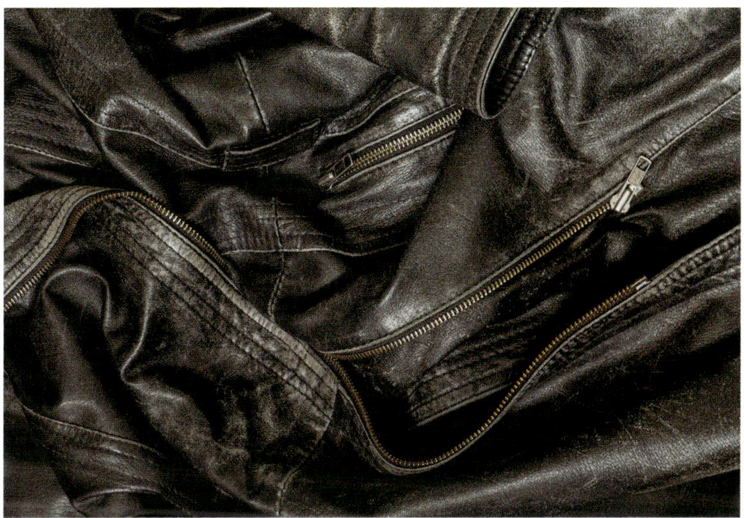

ILLUSTRATION 1.9 W. Carter, *A Black Worn Leather Jacket Made by Jofama AB in Malung, Sweden*, photograph, 2018. Licensed under CC 1.0.

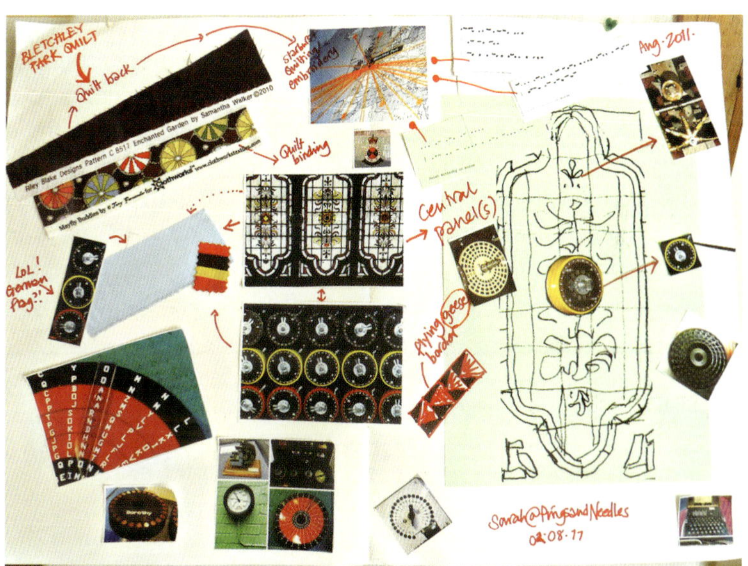

ILLUSTRATION 1.10 Sarah Witherby, *Bletchley Park Quilt – Concept Board*, mixed media, 2011. Licensed under CC BY-SA 2.0.

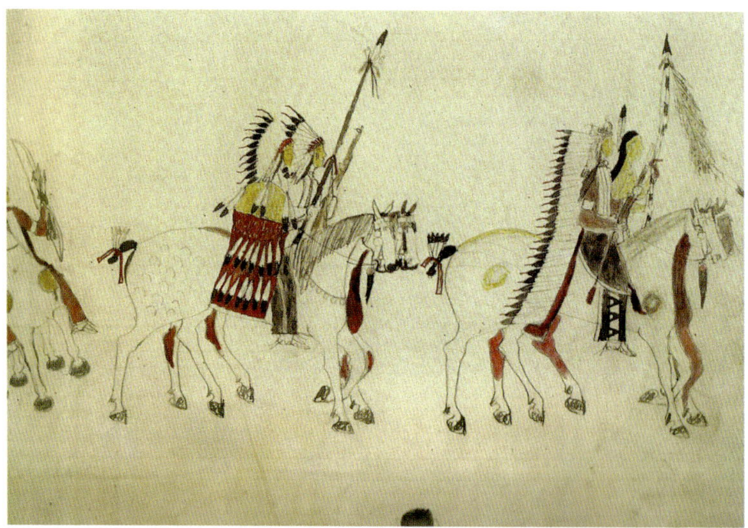

ILLUSTRATION 1.11 Amos Bad Heart Bull, *Battle of Little Bighorn, Montana, USA, 25–26 June 1876*, ink on paper, 1900.

The relationship between observation and memory dominated the teaching and learning of drawing in the West until the twentieth century. This process is no longer dominant but remains one of a number of historic methods still in use. The drawing student divides their activities between making observational drawings and copying existing drawings. The activity of copying existing drawings is thought to connect students with the accumulated knowledge that an existing drawing contains. First, the student tries to reproduce the ways in which an older drawing has been made. Through this process, they are expected to become familiar with the **craft** skills that were employed

CRAFT Craft is a body of knowledge producing learned capacities (skills) within particular circumstances. Although craft is associated with manual skills, manual manipulation and making (such as drawing, playing a musical instrument, writing or blacksmithing), techniques for gaining and making use of manual knowledge are now also applied to any learned capacities, such as game playing, mental arithmetic or theorization.

by the original drafter. Second, the student drafter also learns how specific types of marks had been used to represent objects or scenes in the past, as shown in the existing drawings they are copying. Vincent van Gogh's (1853–1890) painted copy of a print by Japanese artist Hiroshige (1797–1858) demonstrates this type of learning by copying (Illustration 1.12).

Imitation of the actions of other drafters, by students, is a process of social learning. With the example of copying an existing drawing, the

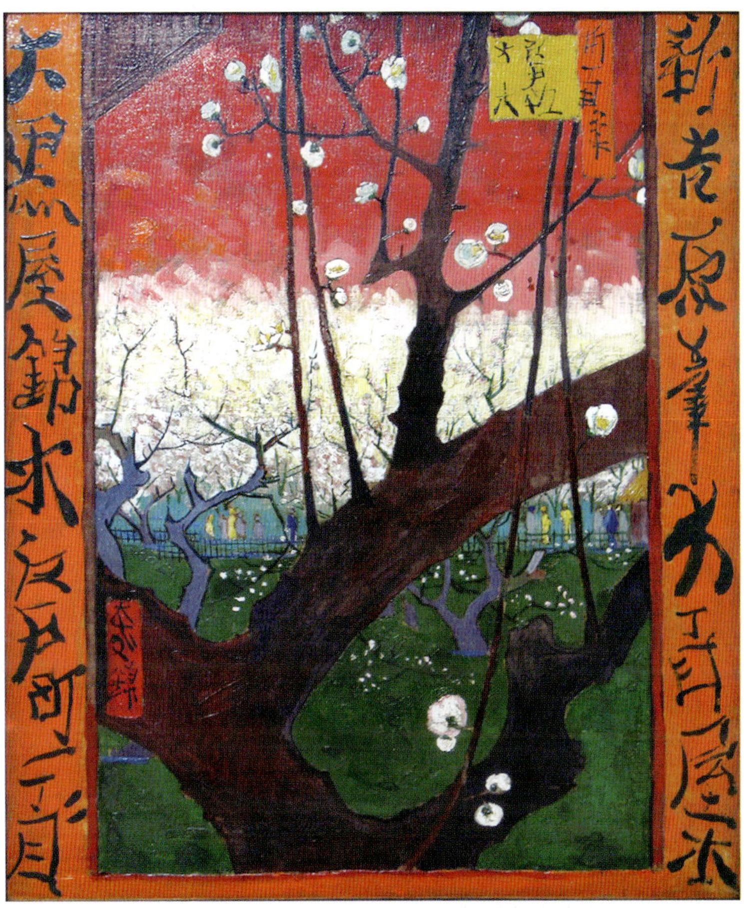

ILLUSTRATION 1.12 Vincent van Gogh, *Flowering Plum Tree (after Hiroshige)*, oil on canvas, 1887. Photograph by artanonymous licensed under CC BY 2.0.

student learns by imitating actions rather than by directly experiencing a scene. This process of learning by imitation is never simply a matter of reproducing the movements of the hand or body, in copying a series of marks. Deeper cognitive and physical processes are rehearsed and remembered. When the student imitates the actions of a past drafter, in making a copy of a drawing, the student also infers the overall goals of the original drafter and makes adjustments to their own actions to try to reach the same goals.

When students learn to draw, copying requires a recalibration of the student's drawing activities, as the student intuits the goals of the original drafter and modifies their own gestures and ideas. Copying represents this learning process. Imitation does not focus on the reproduction of a drawing as an object but on inference and the modification of the process of making the drawn copy.

As the student attempts to understand the original drafter's intention, by comparing their own drawing with the original, they have to recalibrate their own expectations and manual skills. The differences between the student's experience of the original drawing and the experience of their own copy, guide this recalibration. These differences challenge the student to intuit the original drafter's intentions and then to understand the differences between the original and their copy.

Alongside these copying activities, in the eighteenth and nineteenth centuries the student drafter was also instructed to make observational drawings, arranging what they could see along strict lines. For example, James Duffield Harding's (1798–1863) *Lessons on Art*, published in 1849, asked students to make progressively more explicit connections between the properties of simple drawn lines or shapes and the properties of objects in the observed world, such as recognizing a curving line on the drawn page as being similar to the visible curve of a bridge (Illustration 1.13).

Both of these activities – directed observation and copying – were the target for the nineteenth century's most radical Western reformer of drawing, John Ruskin (1819–1900). Ruskin correctly identified that copying aimed to help the student to make drawings that imitated other drawings. Further, he saw that the types of strictly directed observation, recommended in most manuals, aimed to train the student to use

61

SECTION III.

LESSON 64. On Curved Objects.

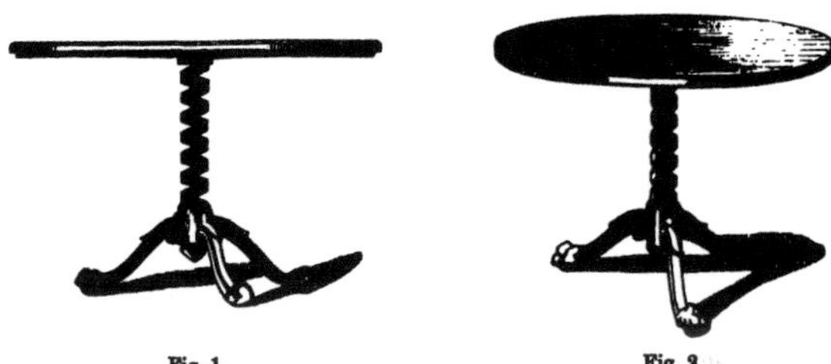

Fig. 1.   Fig. 2.

143. Stoop down so as to bring your eye on a level with a round table, and the top of it will appear a straight line, as in Fig. 1; as you rise, the table top will no longer appear a straight line, but a curve, as in Fig. 2.   The more a curved object is below the eye, the wider its curves will be, as may be seen in Fig. 4, where the bottom part curves much more than the top.   If the part is above the eye, then the lines will appear to curve over, as in Fig. 3.   Again, if a cylinder be placed horizontally and opposite to the eye, the middle part will appear a

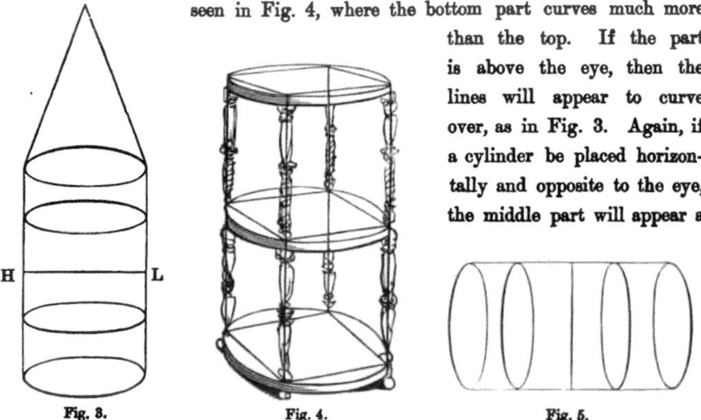

Fig. 3.   Fig. 4.   Fig. 5.

vertical line, as in Fig. 5; and the portions to the right and left respectively will appear as vertical curves, widening as they get more to the right or left.

F

ILLUSTRATION 1.13 James Duffield Harding, *Lessons on Art*, 1849.

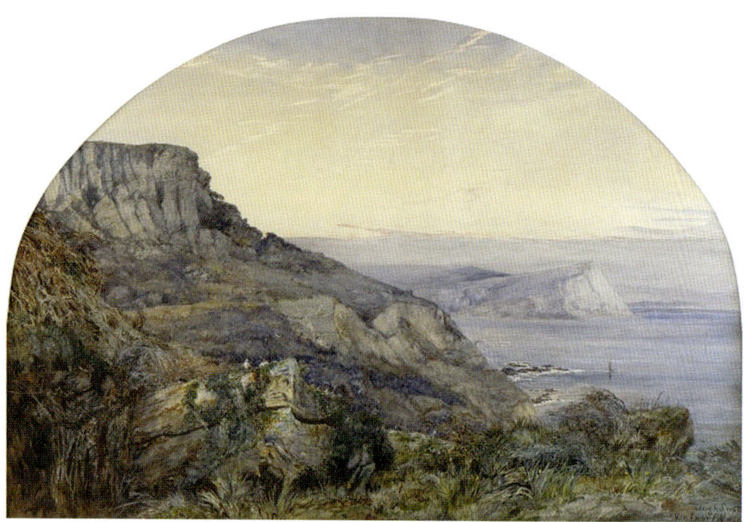

ILLUSTRATION 1.14 Barbara Bodichon, *Ventnor, Isle of Wight*, watercolour and gouache on paper, 1857.

established types of marks, to imitate what the drafter could see. In *The Elements of Drawing, in Three Letters to Beginners*, published in 1857, he attacked both copying and directed observation as methods of teaching drawing. He proposed that the student drafter should amalgamate free observational drawing with emotional responses to the scene in view, starting each drawing as though it is the first drawing ever made and ignoring the guidance of imposed instructions or shared craft knowledge (Illustration 1.14).

In some respects, Ruskin returned to Plato in this. Plato described the purpose of drawing as visual imitation, but he also proposed that visual appearances depend entirely upon the point from which a view is taken. In imitating appearances, a drafter is recording a relationship with appearances, and rarely provides a visual imitation that simply encompasses and substitutes the object that is being drawn.

In fact, in *The Elements of Drawing*, Ruskin proposed that drawing both imitates what can be seen and creates a new visual reality. In attempting to imitate the visible world, he wrote, drawings always fall short. However, in falling short, they also contribute to that visible world. The relationship between what can be seen and what is drawn represents a new understanding of the visible world. This is the drafter's point of view.

In this sense, visual imitation constitutes a type of knowledge about what is seen, alongside other types of knowledge, such as experiences of the drawing medium. Knowledge gained by visual scrutiny does not itself produce illusions, or drawings that are mistaken for their object. Rather, imitation is always judged against a range of benchmarks. These include the purpose to which a drawing will be put or social conventions of taste, which also guide the placing and type of marks. These benchmarks determine how imitative a drawing is judged to be, as much as the presentation of marks designed to reproduce a motionless, **monocular** image.

MONOCULAR Literally, 'one-eyed'. Human vision is binocular, that is, produced by two eyes. Monocular vision establishes clues for the recognition of depth that have historically favoured the use of spatial projection systems to make two-dimensional representations of three-dimensional objects, offering and representing a single point of view.

Untrained drafters often draw what they know about a scene rather than what they can see. For example, suppose that an untrained drafter knows that a car has four wheels and ensures that their drawing shows four wheels. Showing four wheels in the drawing represents the drafter's knowledge of the car, even if all four wheels are not always visible when they look at a car, depending on their point of view. The untrained drafter does not use visual point of view to guide their drawing. They use other knowledge of the car (Illustration 1.15).

On the other hand, according to this untrained method, trained drafters make inaccurate drawings because they draw what they can see rather than what they know. We all know that a car has four wheels, but a trained drafter will only draw what can been seen, even if that means that their drawing of a car only shows two wheels, when we know it has four (Illustration 1.16).

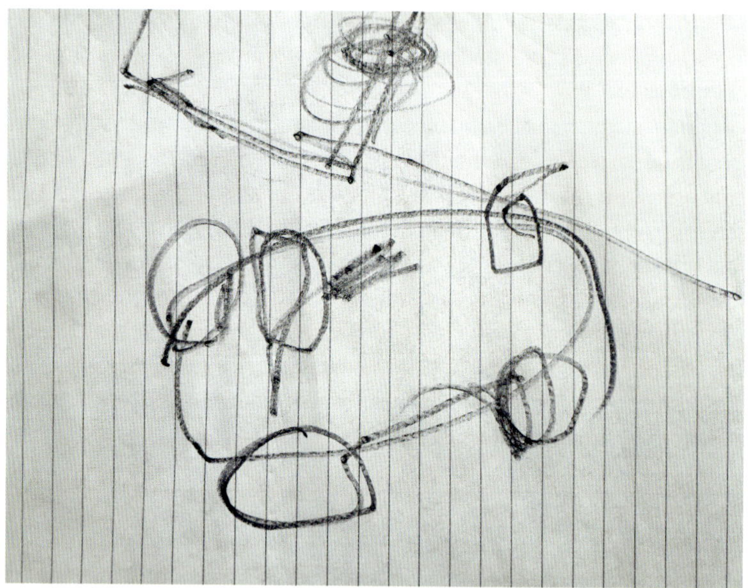

ILLUSTRATION 1.15 Anonymous, *Car*, ink on paper, 2019.

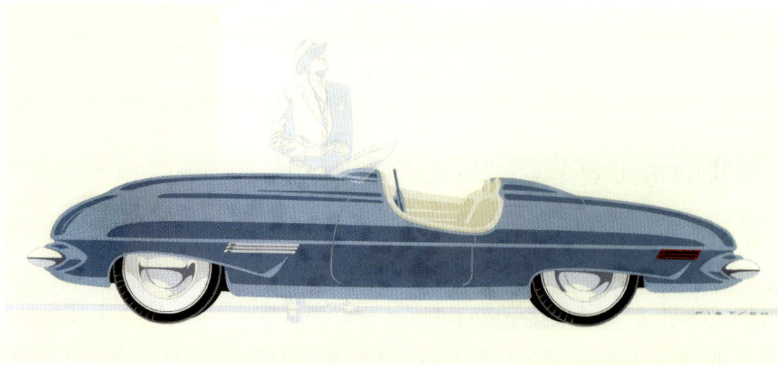

ILLUSTRATION 1.16 T. W. Pietsch II, *Blue Roadster*, gouache on paper, 1944.

Digital imitation

Very recently, in the history of visual imitation, the direct relationship between the properties of a medium and the properties of the scene or object that it imitates has been disturbed further by the introduction of digital technology. With analogue media, such as paper and pen, a drawn mark becomes significant through a direct relationship between its properties and properties in the scene it seeks to represent. This direct relationship is analogous. For example, the colour of a mark is the same as the colour of the object it represents. A yellow mark might indicate a banana or a shaft of yellow sunlight, because all of these things share the property 'yellow'. However, digital technology interposes between the mark and its object by re-coding it as a series of values, zero or one, which accumulate in different sequences to create commands.

Although it seems rather counterintuitive, this re-coding has provided the means by which a coded mark can be perfectly reproduced. Every copy of a digital mark is an identical reproduction of the code that produces it. Its properties are exactly the same. On the other hand, the properties of analogue imitations change when they are submitted to any processes of reproduction. For example, a photocopy of a drawing has quite different properties to the original drawing. A digital copy and its original are identical because they make use of the same code, whereas a copy of an analogue mark always displays different properties, even in the same medium. If imitation is a type of representation, digital technology is peerless in imitating representations (Illustration 1.17).

Analogue imitation

Digital media do not find significance in any residual traces left by the drafter's body. Traces of the drafter's body, on the other hand, are thought of as fundamentally significant with analogue media. According to this distinction, between digital and analogue copies, these residual traces are the source of any likeness that a drawing has to the object that the drawing represents. This is because (the argument goes) visible, residual traces recreate the bodily actions of the drafter for the viewer whilst also encompassing the material properties of the object of the drawing.

In analogue drawing, the particular properties of the movement of the drafter's hand creates the particular properties (the shape, size and density) of the drawn mark and these are also shared with the properties

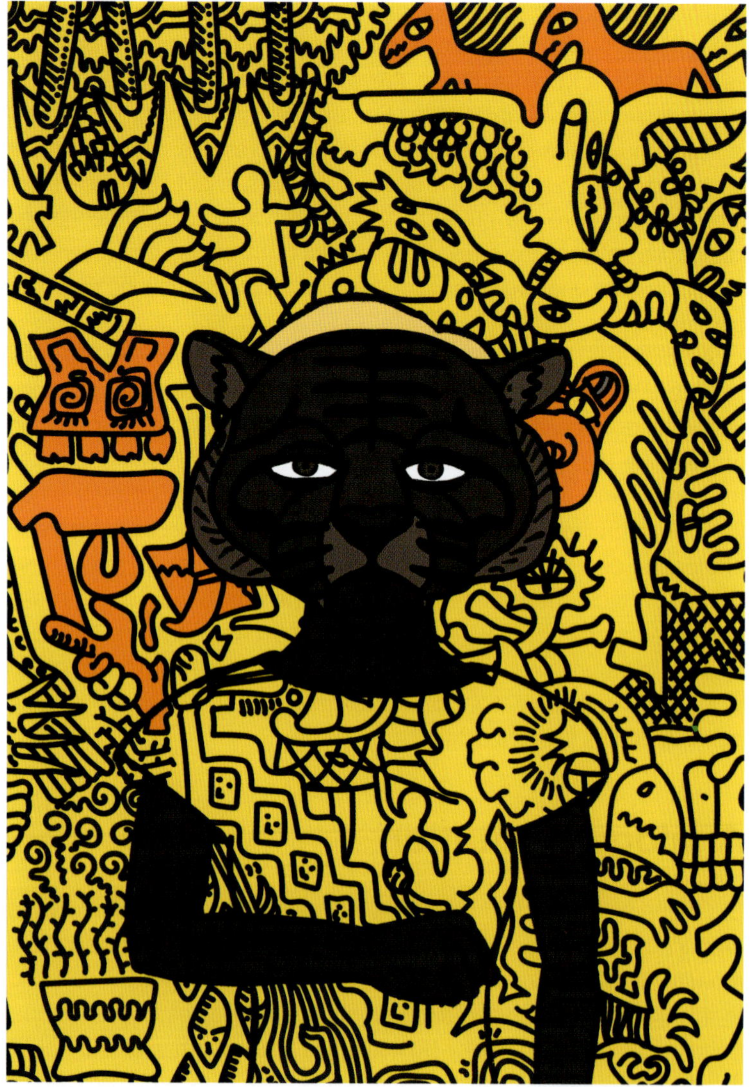

ILLUSTRATION 1.17 Suum Cuique Labs GmbH, *An example of hashmask image that accompanies a Non-Fungible Token (NFT)*, digital, 2021.

of the part of the scene or object that the mark describes. These three stages of imitation can be recognized in any drawing. We frequently use the same adjective to describe the character of what is drawn, the materials used and how it is drawn. For example, a wobbly hand traces a wobbly line depicting a wobbly part of a scene. The wobble is considered to be the same for hand, mark and scene (Illustration 1.18).

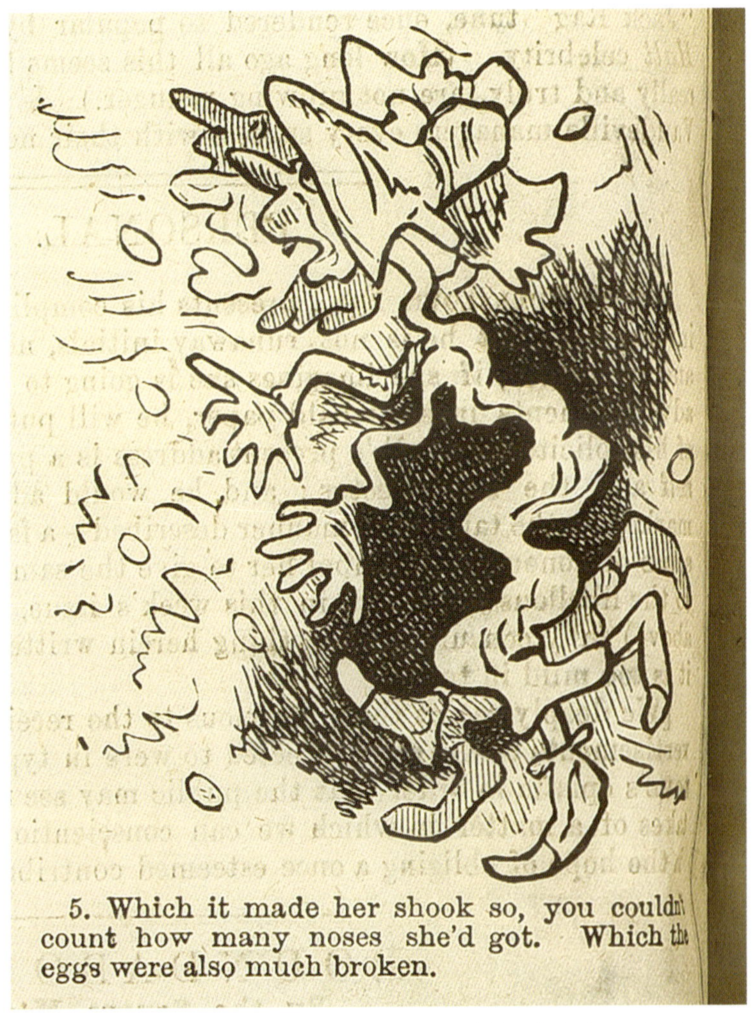

ILLUSTRATION 1.18 Marie Duval, 'Ghost-esses' (detail) *Judy, or the London Serio-comic Journal*, wood engraving, 1873.

Imitating experience

An alternative, more recent, approach shifts the terms upon which imitation is adjudicated, from vision to experience. According to this approach, the function of drawing is to imitate (perhaps conjure would be a more accurate word) aspects of an object, occurrence, scene or emotion that are invisible, that is, perceived by other means than sight. On this basis, when the emotional sensation for a viewer, prompted by a drawing, resembles emotional sensations derived elsewhere, then an imitation has been achieved – not of visible properties but of invisible ones.

However, this shift in the purpose of imitation, to imitate experiences rather than to imitate appearances, reintroduces the significance of a range of possible types of experience as a source for drawings, beyond what is seen. As with the exercise for drawing students, copying existing drawings, imitation does not necessarily entail the reproduction of appearances. Instead, the present-time experience of the drafter is imitated. This type of drawing activity focuses on sharing the process of imitation by making use of an original as a prop in a rehearsal.

This type of emotional imitation was also an idea discussed by Plato, albeit in the context of reaching emotional truth in theatre performances rather than in drawing. However, in this discussion, Plato acknowledges a distinction between theatrical performance and verbal oration because theatre is a visual as well as a verbal medium. Theatre both shows visual images and tells verbal stories. The boundaries between the two are overcome through emotional imitation. Plato describes this as a process in which artists and audiences conspire to imitate a shared emotional experience. This is also the model for drawings that imitate emotions by rehearsing them.

Michael Taussig (b.1940) takes further this idea of imitation as a process of emotional participation. He claims that artists and audiences are mutually 'touched' by shared representations that imitate emotional experiences. The metaphor of touch is very appropriate for imitative drawings that are made in this way – that is, by touching a surface to make a mark. For example, for the student copyist, imitation turns out to be a process of creating formal analogies for shared emotional experiences. Viewers of drawings might be thought of as also undertaking this process of sharing imitated emotions by looking rather than touching. In Käthe Kollwitz's (1867–1945) drawing, the viewer follows the drafter in rehearsing the emotion represented. The drawing has been made explicitly to set up this situation rather than to imitate the visual appearance of a specific scene at a specific moment. The drawing is not an imitation of the appearance of a scene but a visual representation of a shared emotion (Illustration 1.19).

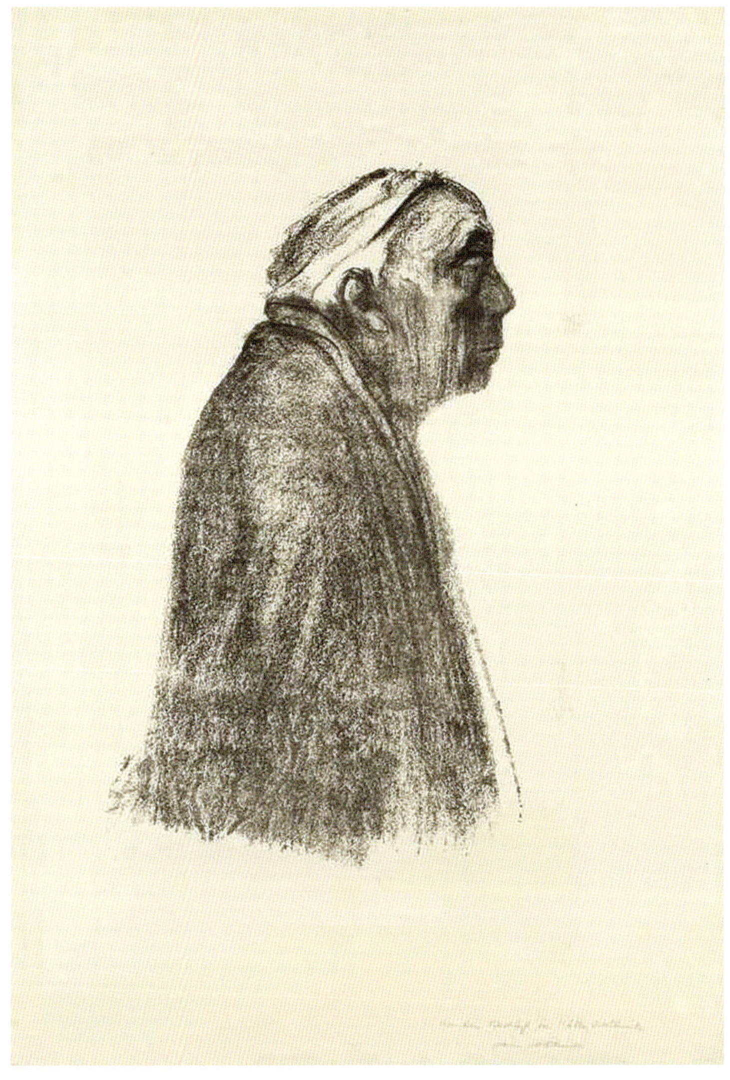

ILLUSTRATION 1.19 Käthe Kollwitz, *Selbstportrat im Profil*, chalk on paper, 1938.

2
MARK

Pietro Aretino's idea, about the significance of materials, also confirmed sixteenth-century distinctions between media, dividing line and colour. Drawing media and painting media were thought of as having distinct characteristics. Drawing media produce a sequence of marks in contrast to the surface on which they are made, the colour of which is relatively insignificant. Painting media produce a skin of blended colours hiding the supporting surface.

In the sixteenth century, the social situations in which drafters and artists used drawing and painting media differed, as well as the media. The situations in which media are employed continue to differ today. For centuries drawing has included a wide range of preparatory plan making and notation as well as works of art. The circumstances in which the craft skills of drawing have been utilized encompass the practical plans produced in engineering workshops and surveys, for example, as well as doodles (the mind maps produced in a thoughtless personal moment), or commercial studios producing magazine illustrations, as well as the preparatory plans buildings or engineering, or for fine art painting and sculpture made in an artist's studio (Illustrations 2.1–2.4).

By establishing the difference between what is shown and how it is shown, Aretino divorced visual media from the imperative to imitate. Although it took a further five centuries for the full implications of this divorce to be understood (with the advent of so-called abstract visual images in the twentieth century), this distinction established an enduring idea of the similarity of all drawing media, across the different situations in which they are used. This distinction placed a strong emphasis upon the visualization of thought processes (such as preparation, planning and doodling) and the visualization of non-visual systems (the best example of which is writing, Illustration 2.5).

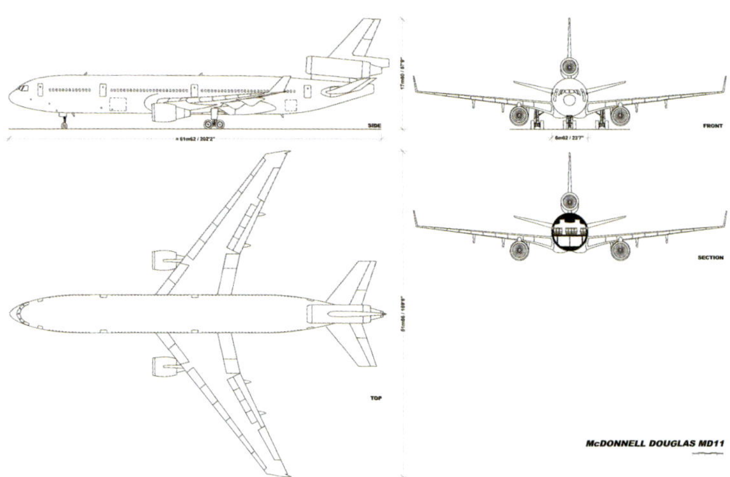

ILLUSTRATION 2.1 Julian Scavini, *Schematics for an MD11*, digital, 2012. Licensed under CC SA 3.0.

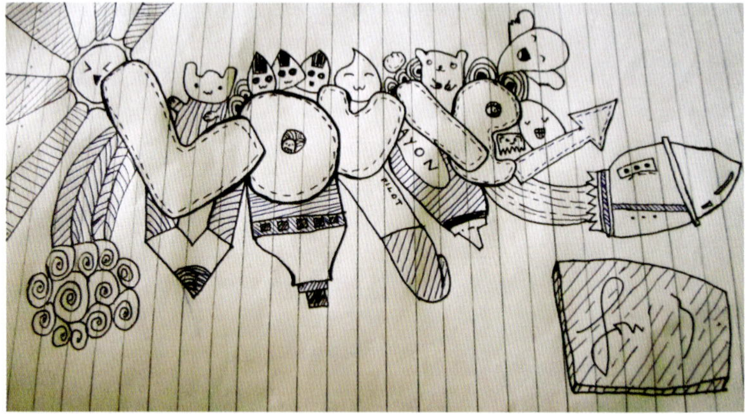

ILLUSTRATION 2.2 Louie Mark, *An Example of a Doodle from the Name Louie*, ink on paper, 2012. Licensed under CC SA 4.0.

Aretino's idea aimed to promote Titian's 'colour' or 'light and air' approach to painting. Indeed, Aretino managed to compare the work of his contemporary, artist Michelangelo Buonarroti (1475–1564), unfavourably to Titian's work because of its 'design' approach. This meant Michelangelo's use of lines to map and demarcate objects

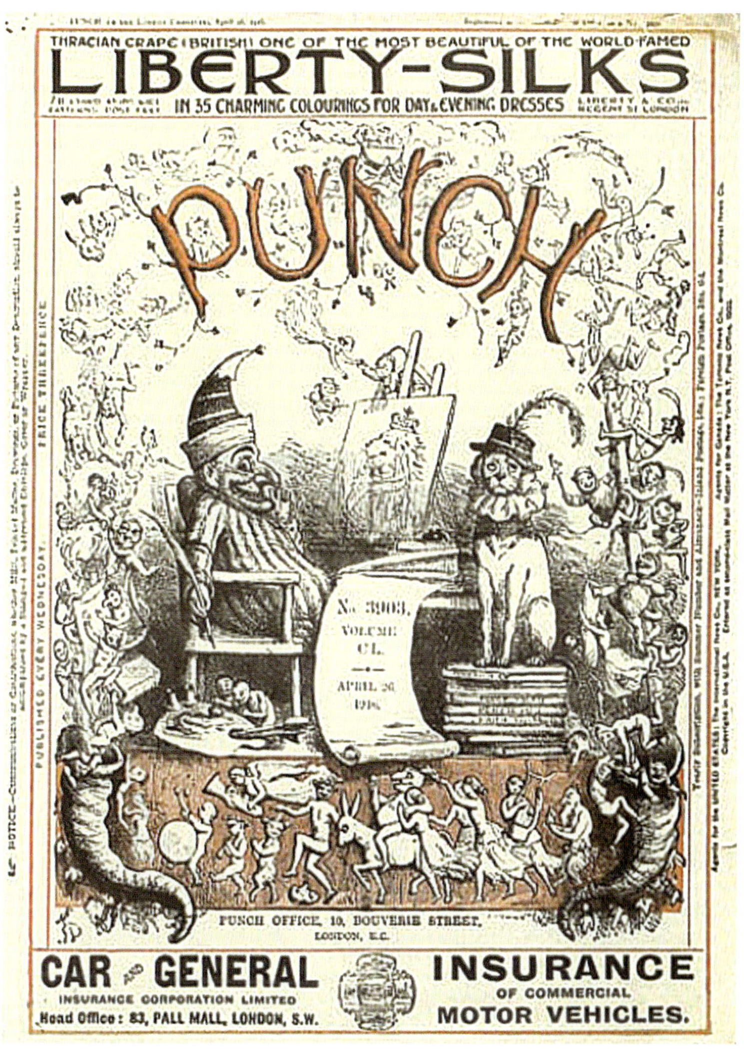

ILLUSTRATION 2.3 Richard Doyle, *Cover of Punch*, engraving, 1916.

in his work as opposed to Titian's use of colour blends to represent atmosphere. Historically, this comparison encompassed the differences between traditions of visual representation and different uses of media, in different regions of Italy (Titian and Aretino being 'Venetian' and Michelangelo 'Florentine') and hence had a political dimension. Aretino

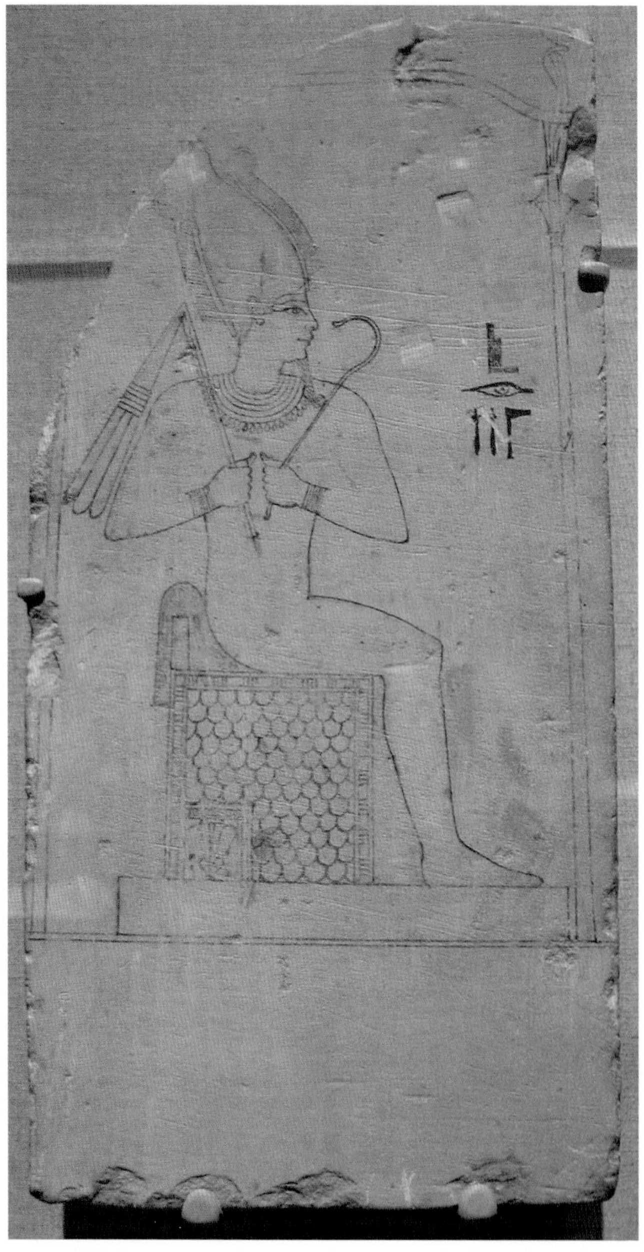

ILLUSTRATION 2.4 Anonymous, *Sketch of Osiris*, limestone, pigment, 305–330 BCE. Brooklyn Museum. Licensed under CC BY 3.0.

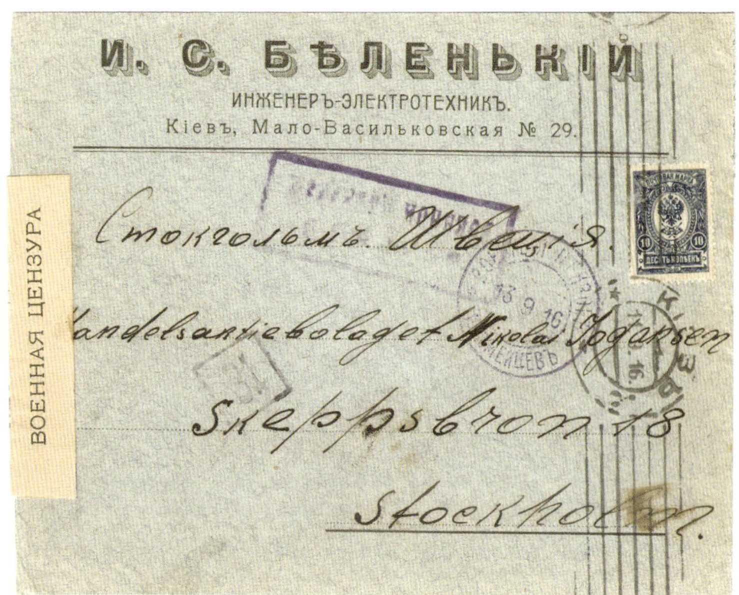

ILLUSTRATION 2.5 Anonymous, censored envelope, ink on paper, 1916.

described Michelangelo as inferior to Titian because he was too much the Florentine drafter and not enough the Venetian artist.

Tone

The tonal value of marks is overwhelmingly significant in drawing, but not necessarily according to Aretino's promotion of the visual representation of atmosphere, as blends of tones or colours. Drawings rely upon tonal contrasts and these contrasts have been viewed in a range of different ways. Similarities between the tone of a mark and the tone of a real-world shadow are simply a shared property of both, despite the fact that one is local to the drawing medium and one is a relative absence of light in a viewed scene. Both share the same visible tone. This shared property has been exploited in the most straightforward of ways: visibly dark objects and environments are depicted with dark drawing materials. The subtlety and variety of this exploitation by drafters is astonishing. It

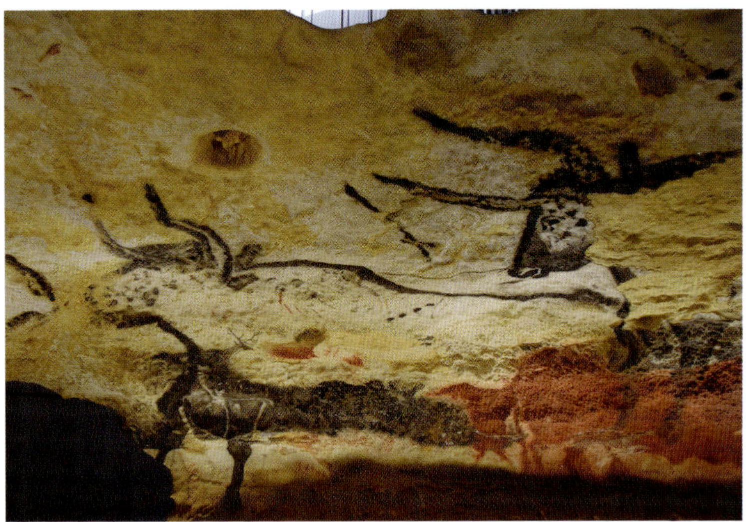

ILLUSTRATION 2.6 Anonymous, *Lascaux IV*, pigment, 17–12 ka. Photograph by Simone Ramella. Licensed under CC BY 2.0.

is shown in very early drawings, such as the prehistoric drawings made by the Magdalenian culture (17–12 ka) at Niaux in France, in which we see darker pigment used to prompt our visualization of both shadows (beneath a bison, for example) and **local** tone (of a bison's mane, for example) (Illustration 2.6).

LOCAL TONE, LOCAL COLOUR The word local is used to describe a tone or colour that is inherent to an object, as opposed to a tone or colour created by atmospheric effects upon objects. An apple might be inherently red (its local colour), whilst appearing pink in early morning light or dark purple at night.

In Jan Van Huysum's (1682–1749) drawing *Bouquet of Flowers in a Terracotta Vase* (1723), tones all show degrees of shadow in a visualized scene. The relative local tones of the flower and vase are similar, but the tonal range of the shadows that describe them is wide. Again, the darker the tone of the mark, the darker the tone of the

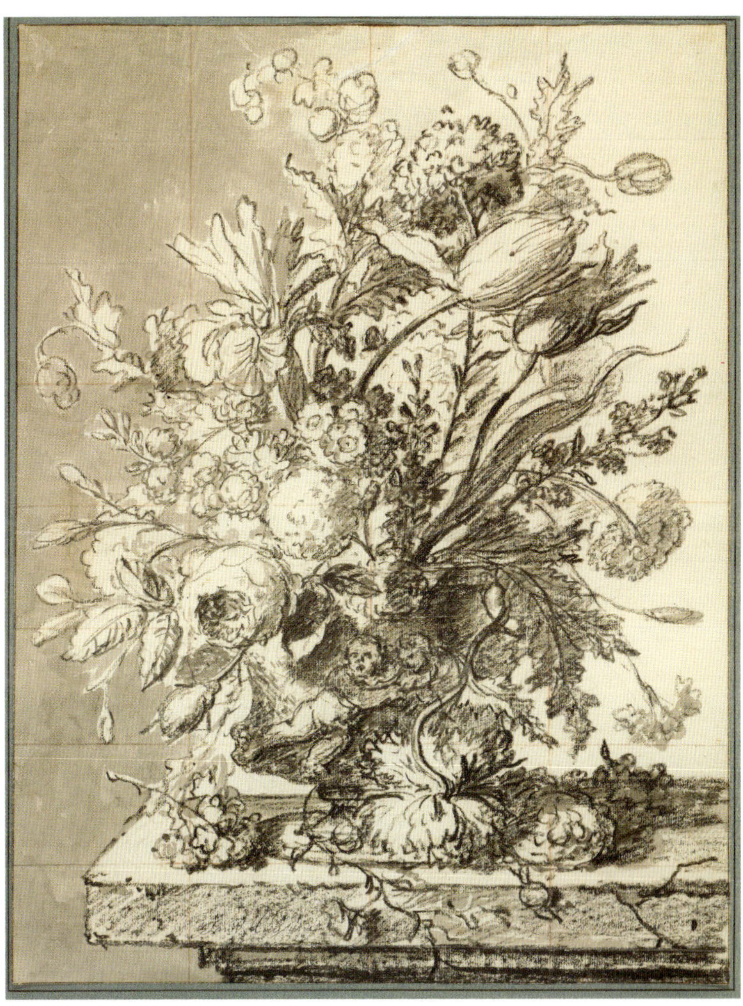

ILLUSTRATION 2.7 Jan Van Huysum, *Bouquet of Flowers in a Terracotta Vase*, pencil on paper, 1723.

shadow (Illustration 2.7). However, in the drawing *Persimmons* (no date), drafter Muqi (1210?–1269?) uses the tone of the mark to show the local tone of each of the fruit, without shadow. Of course, both of these approaches result from experiences of light. The first makes use of the similar properties of shadow and drawing material and the

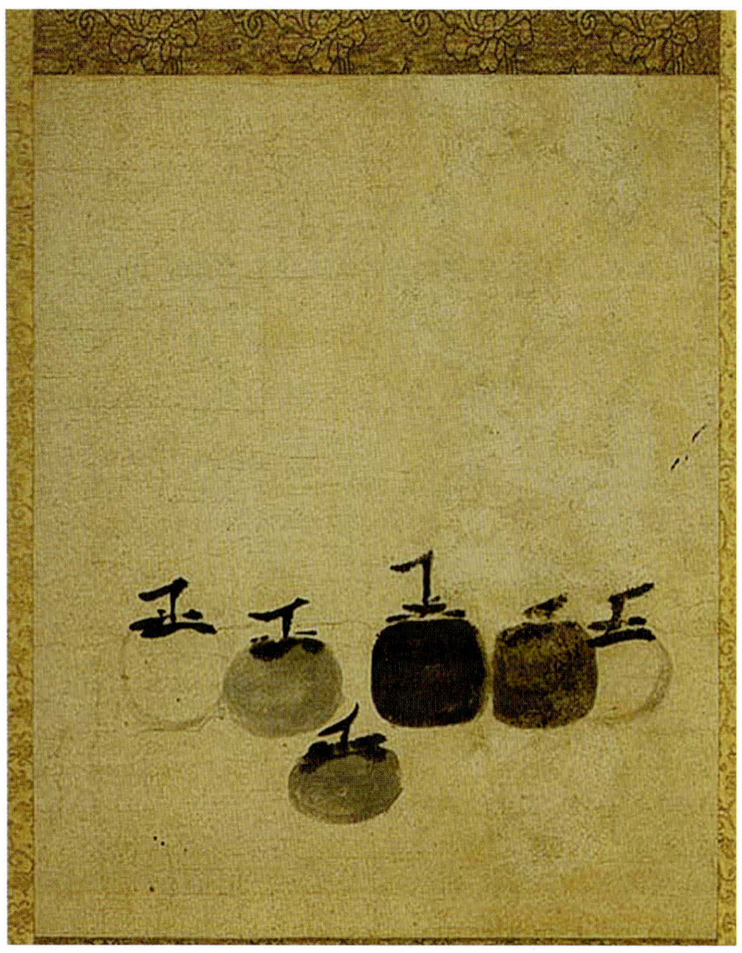

ILLUSTRATION 2.8 Muqi, *Persimmons*, ink on paper, no date.

second makes use of the similarity of the local tone of the depicted object and the drawing material (Illustration 2.8). Artist Garrett Phelan (b.1965) further exploits the fact that dark environments can be depicted with dark materials by using them to make drawn architectural interventions in which it appears that his drawing material is a shadow, in drawings such as *At what point will common sense prevail* (2008) (Illustration 2.9).

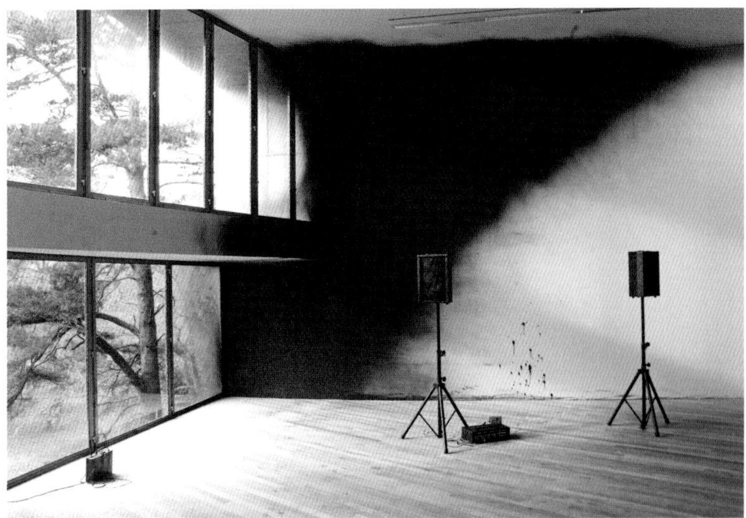

ILLUSTRATION 2.9 Garrett Phelan, *At what point will common sense prevail*, charcoal, 2008. Lewis Glucksman Gallery, Cork, Ireland. Photograph by Matthew Packer. Image courtesy of Garrett Phelan.

Line

The description of drawn marks as lines represents another lasting historic association, which is still so strong as to sometimes be considered a definition of drawing. A line is two things. First, it is an abstract idea, representing two dimensions, extending the idea of a one-dimensional point. Neither point nor line has any material manifestation. They are ideas. A point is the idea of a location in space and a line is the idea of either an accumulation of adjacent points or the distance between two remote points. Second, however, line is also a trace of the direction in which the drafter forces the drawing medium, the material making a mark. But the variety of drawings is not limited to either the idea of the line or by any single direction of travel of the drawing medium.

For example, the act of drafting a line is understood in anthropology as a way for an anthropologist to gain incremental knowledge of the object of the drawing. The line is considered to be a record of a process of gaining knowledge. The more an anthropologist draws, the more they know about the objects of their drawing, their relationships with it,

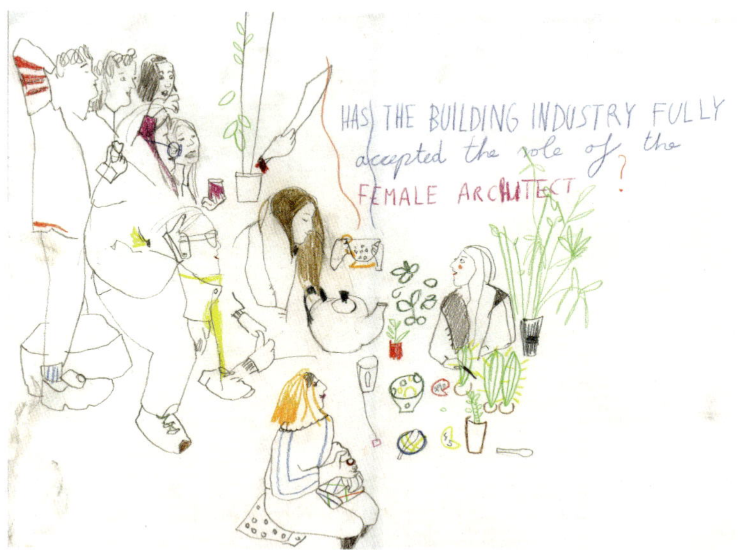

ILLUSTRATION 2.10 Judit Ferencz, *Has the Building Industry Fully Accepted the Role of the Female Architect?* pencil on paper, 2018.

and the more they are familiar with the process of gaining knowledge (Illustration 2.10). As we have seen, the line is an idea rather than a component of a technical process or the visualization of an image. It frequently represents an idea of motion, or the **force dynamics**, required to produce a change in location in comparison to a frame of reference. For the anthropologist who draws, this motion is the process of gaining accumulated knowledge. For drafters with other aims, the

---

FORCE DYNAMICS Force dynamics are measures and types of energy, generated by making comparisons with other forces, as environmental features. For example, mass, size and motion are categories of time and space that are often thought of as resources that every body makes use of (how fast, strong, large or old a body is). When a force is applied, mass is a property of comparative resistance to changes in motion. Motion is a change in location in comparison to a frame of reference. Size is abstracted from comparative judgements of magnitude.

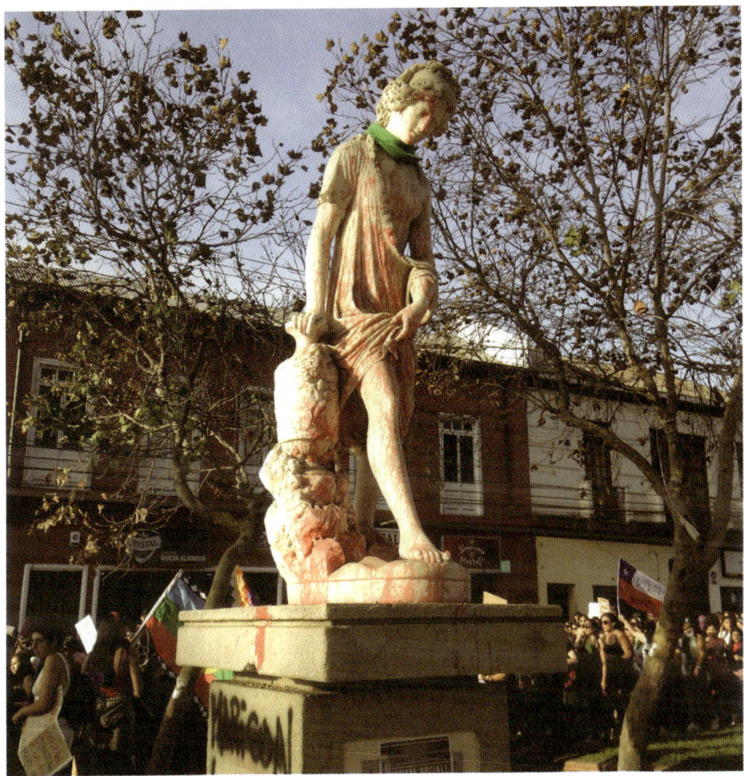

ILLUSTRATION 2.11 Valeria Rojas Bruja, *Sculpture of the Open Air Museum of La Serena with a feminist handkerchief and with stains representing the injured protesters at the hands of the Chilean Police*, paint, fabric, 2020. Licensed under CC SA 4.0.

force dynamics of the mobile line are often used to bring about changes in the world rather than to gain knowledge of it. The splashes of paint and tied fabric applied by the Chilean artist Valeria Rojas Bruja to nineteenth-century statues of women use the dynamics of the splashed lines to visually contradict and call into question existing social ideas (Illustration 2.11).

Motion is, in fact, an experience of displacement. The line prompts the idea of this displacement and, as a result, provides the evidence for it. This is what artist Paul Klee (1879–1940) meant when he is said to have written that the drawn line 'goes for a stroll' (the attribution of these words to him is unproved, but they are often repeated). The frames of reference against which motion is perceived are always defined relative to the resources that are made available by our bodies. In the case of experiences of motion, these include velocity, acceleration, duration, speed, distance or relative proximity, rhythm and sequence. All of these types of motion directly prompt emotional reactions and social responses.

Hence, degrees of velocity, acceleration and the rest are always present as properties of the drafter's body. For centuries, drawing teachers have instructed students that a mark made from the shoulder is different to a mark made from the wrist and that a mark made from the wrist is different to a mark made from the fingers. It is easy to imagine the broad, bold, fast arc of a mark made from the shoulder, where 'broad', 'bold' and 'fast' are defined in relation to the body of the drafter and the body of the viewer. The Japanese artist Hokusai (1760–1849) famously made a monumental ink drawing of the monk Daruma to demonstrate the spectacular use of his whole body, to make a drawing (Illustration 2.12). Compare this with the 'narrow', 'delicate' and 'slow' touch of a mark made from the thumb and first finger (Illustration 2.13). The properties of each type of movement and each type of mark derive from the specific characteristics of motion as a potential resource of the drafter's body.

A range of commonplace ways in which we make sense of our physical experiences easily evidences this idea. We often imagine the single dimension in which lines occur as either physical material or dynamic force. This is what occurs when we draw imaginary lines on an imaginary plane between stars to make a 'constellation', or when we see any horizon. In both cases, our bodily experience is the definitive source upon which our imagined lines depend. We commonly consider the night sky as still and flat (flat enough to be imagined as a single dimension on which we draw constellations). This is because we do not experience the dynamics of cosmic space, we experience the dynamics of our own bodies. The horizon is an imaginary boundary (the furthest distance we can see), which only moves when we change the location of our bodies.

We usually think of these bodily resources as shared, general and commonplace, in the sense that human physiology is shared. In fact, human physiology is not necessarily shared, general and commonplace at all. Our potential experiences of our own bodies, our ideas about them, and the bodies of others are not necessarily shared, nor have they necessarily been shared in the past. Bodily resources are

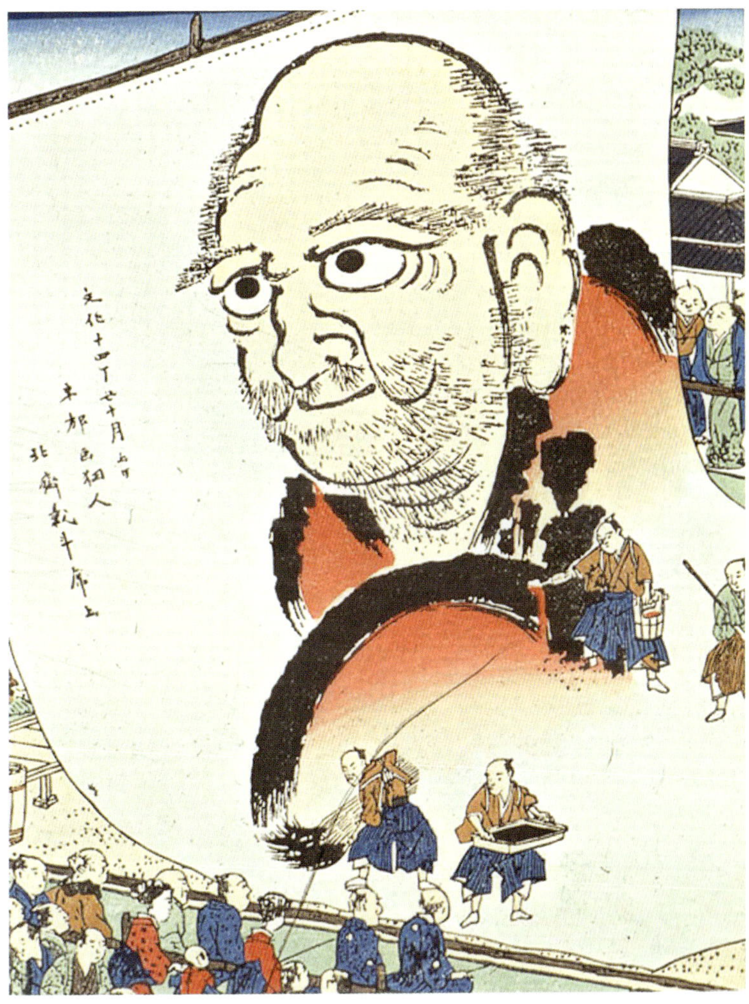

ILLUSTRATION 2.12 Katsushika Hokusai, *Hokusai painting the Great Daruma at Honganji Nagoya Betsuin (Nishi-Honganji) in 1817*, woodcut, 1817.

profound and highly calibrated, because they are as various as human experience is various. The range of ways in which we might imagine a line demonstrates the range of potential resources of the body.

For example, Aboriginal Australian cosmology imagines the Australian continent to be crossed by directional force lines that evidence the paths of the ancestors who created it. Sailors in Polynesia notate experiences

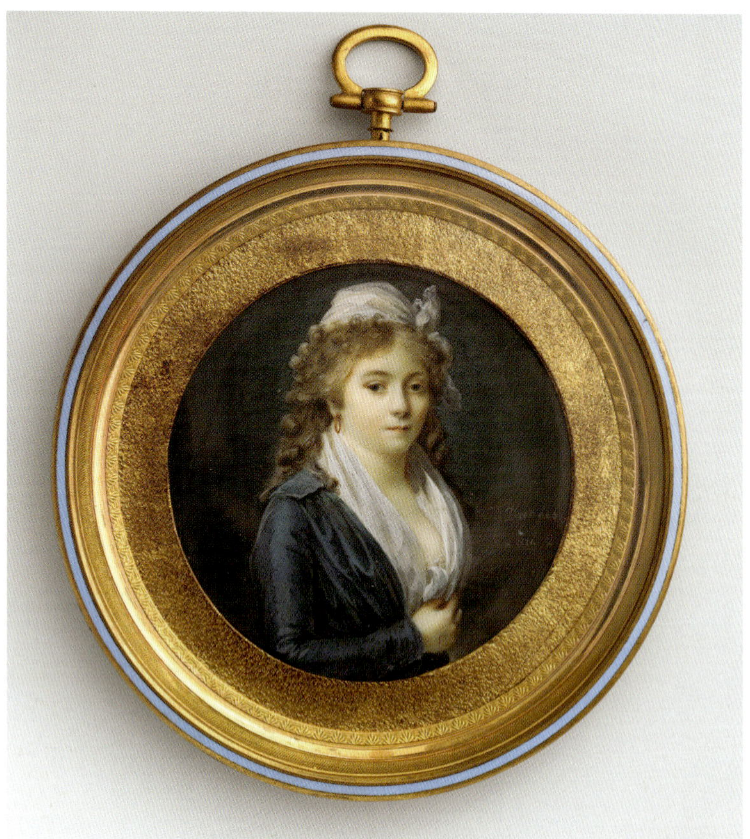

ILLUSTRATION 2.13 Frédéric Dubois, *Portrait of a Woman*, watercolour, 1794.

of the directions of the seascape passed down over hundreds of years (Illustration 2.14). These lines give character to both geographic features, to conceptions of time and to the unfolding sequences of creation stories. Drafters derive these ideas of lines from their bodily experiences, including their traditions of living. For people with other bodily experiences and other potential ideas, such as Europeans, these lines are unlikely to be features of a landscape.

A similar relationship between specific bodily experiences and an idea about lines guides the teaching of writing skills in modern China. Children learn to write by first gesturing the ways in which the characters will be written whilst naming the marks that make them and then

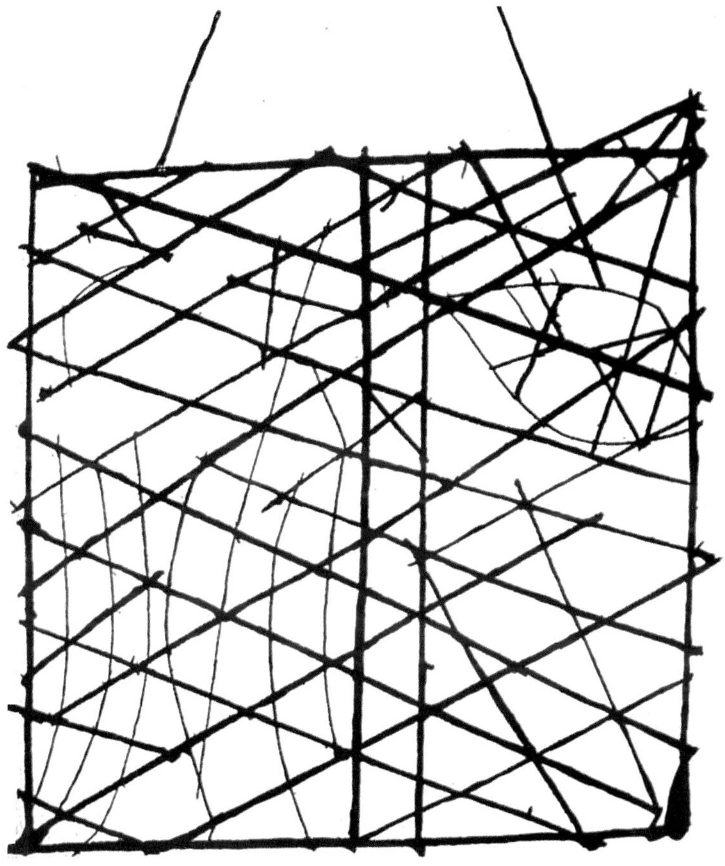

ILLUSTRATION 2.14 Polynesian navigation device showing directions of winds, waves and islands, 1904.

pronouncing the character's name. The choreography of sequences and types of gestures, made by imagining the lines of writing performed in air, ultimately guides the replication of the same gestures whilst holding an implement that leaves a trace of these gestures, a brush or pen full of ink. Whilst these learning activities are often described according to the media that they use (such as brush and ink), the popular Chinese pastime of 'water calligraphy' shows the whole range of the body gestures brought into being by this idea of the line. The water evaporates, leaving no trace. The drawing is as ephemeral as the

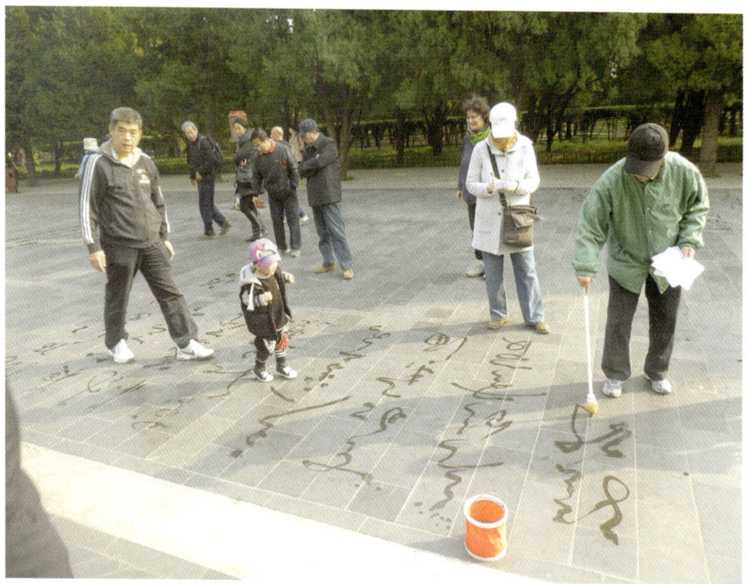

ILLUSTRATION 2.15 Immanuel Giel, *Water calligraphy*, photograph, 2009. Licensed under CC SA 4.0.

gesture that produced it (Illustration 2.15). In these Chinese classrooms, the naming of marks and characters is first the naming of the gestures that need to be performed to make them, or the focusing of specific bodily resources according to an idea of the line.

Planning

The Chinese method of teaching students to write by training them to produce preliminary gestures belongs to a tradition in which mark making itself is part of a chain of activities rather than an end result. In particular, this includes traditions of making drawings as plans and models, which collate knowledge and transform this knowledge for future use. All so-called technical drawings evidence this idea of mark making, such as drawing for engineering, design, architecture and manufacturing processes (Illustration 2.16). In these examples, drawings are made to collate and systematically present knowledge that has already be gained and classified. The marks making up this

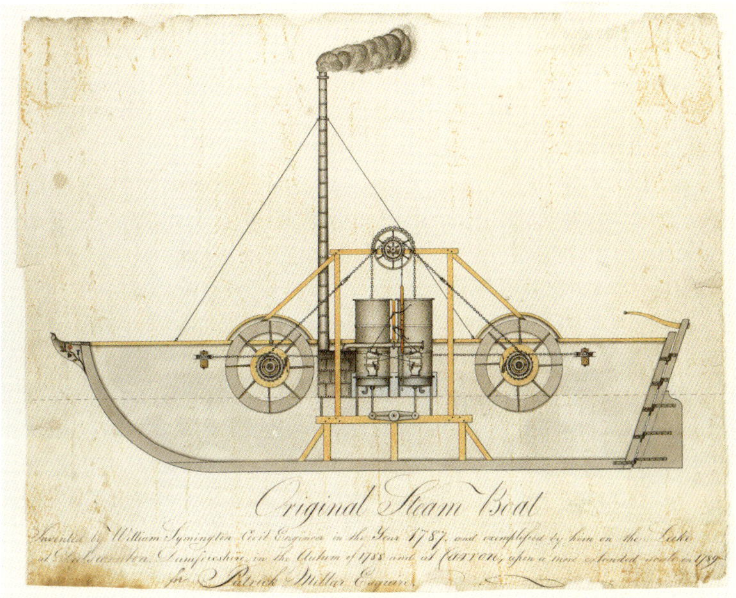

ILLUSTRATION 2.16 William Symington, *Original Steam Boat for Patrick Miller Esq*, 1787–1788. Museums Victoria. Licensed under CC PDM 1.0.

type of drawing are directed by the aim of enabling a future task or tasks. They make use of **symbolic** representations, positioned relative to each other, where the relative size and location of each symbol is guided by a system of relationships within the drawing that correspond to specific relationships outside the drawing.

SYMBOL A symbol is a type of sign that makes use of a learned set of conventions. These conventions dictate that the sign means something, that it is agreed that 'this' means 'that'. Symbols differ from two other types of sign, indexical signs, which make a physical connection between the sign and what it signifies, and iconic signs, which resemble what they signify.

The recognition of the identity, complexity and status of drawings made to direct future activities came late to the fine arts, in the twentieth century. The preparatory drawings made by visual artists occasionally gained the status of a work of art, but these drawings are not to be confused with the use of conventional drawing media to make finished artworks. They are quite different. Hence, the great impact of the 1966 exhibition *Working Drawings and Other Visible Things on Paper not Necessarily Meant to be Viewed as Art* at the School of the Visual Arts, New York. This exhibition included drawings made to facilitate scientific processes, architectural plans, mathematical diagrams, preliminary sketches, invoices and letters, and engineering drawings.

The exhibition articulated the idea that the identity of drawings like these is overwhelmed by their function as plans. Outside the contexts in which they are used, they are invisible. The exhibition argued that planning and modelling drawings make visible the social and material relationships that demand their production. In particular, it highlighted the long-standing use of planning drawings in two and three dimensions, in architecture, engineering and medical science, where the degree of risk of failure of buildings, machines and procedures is lessened by the use of drawn plans and models. These types of drawings reveal that works of art are also made through similar processes of planning. To the art world, the exhibition revealed facts that professional drafters had known for centuries, across many disciplines. Drawing is very often a rational and preconceived activity rather than the expression of personal emotion or individual genius. The exhibition pointed to the fact that drawing activities have a long relationship with analytical thinking, logic and the production and use of systems.

Mapping

Maps are also drawings made as plans for use, utilizing systematically organized symbols. The drafter and viewer of a map share an understanding that a specifically located symbol is substituted for a distinct feature, or another experience, like a road, hill or river, for example. In the visual symbolic system used in British Ordnance Survey geographical maps, a square with an oblique triangle and the letter 'M' substitutes for a museum and a silhouette of a fairground horse substitutes for an entertainment attraction (Illustration 2.17). Beyond

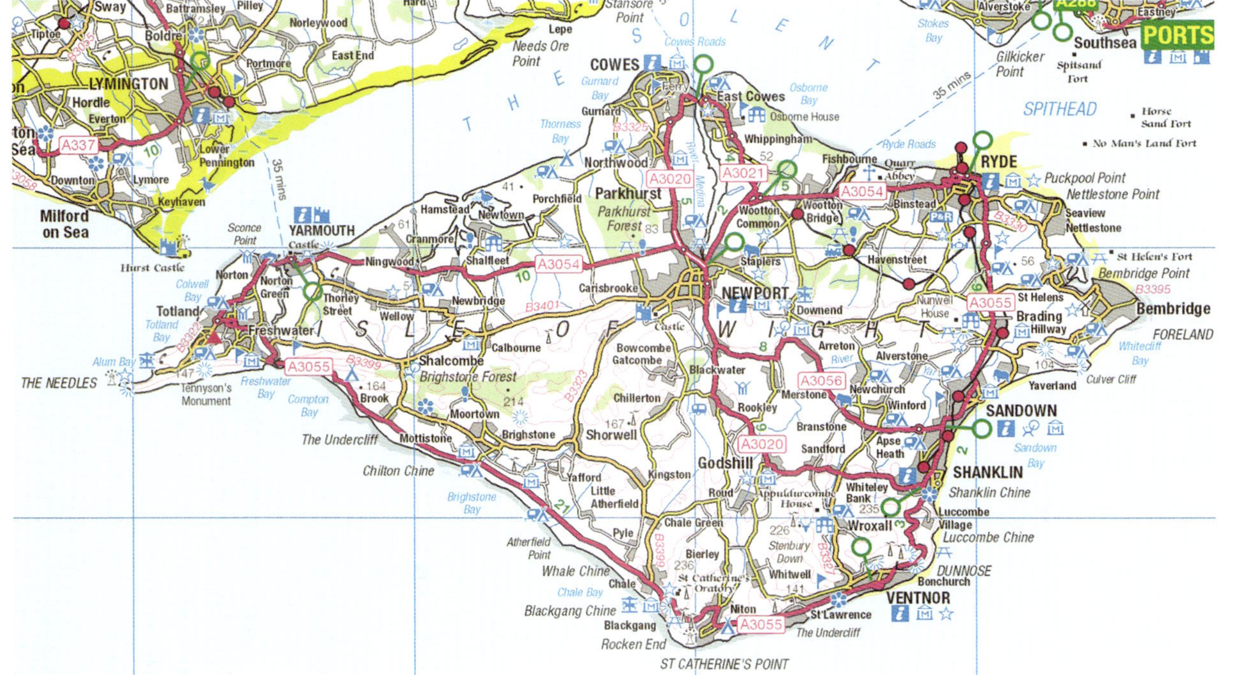

ILLUSTRATION **2.17** Ordnance Survey, *Map of the Isle of Wight*, digital, 2020. Contains Ordnance Survey data © Crown copyright and database right.

this, however, the use of symbolic images in maps only becomes meaningful within an overarching system that determines the location of each symbol relative to others.

Maps, then, are types of drawings in which the location and type of marks correspond to something else – what the drawing is a map of. In other words, the relative location of the array of marks on a surface, plus the differences between repeated types of marks corresponds to relationships that appear in the real world.

These relationships, between symbols and between the locations of symbols, can be both systematic and unsystematic. With systematic correspondences between the drawn map and what it maps, there is a governing relationship between the treatment of an item in the map and its place as part of an external experience. This is easily understood in a scale relationship, where a degree of distance between items on the map systematically represents another degree of distance on, say, the ground. If a distance of one centimetre on a drawing represents a distance of one kilometre on the ground, then two centimetres must equal two kilometres. The scale ruler from Rocque's *Map of the British Isles* shows how two different scale systems on the ground (English and Irish) were systematically equivalent to the same distance on the map (Illustration 2.18). If a drawn cross in one part of the drawing represents a place of worship, then so must a cross in another part of the drawing. Drawings that make use of systems are among the most well-known geographical drawn maps, such as those employing the system devised by Gerardus Mercator (1512–1594) or the system devised by James Gall (1808–185) and finalized by Arno Peters (1916–2002) (Illustrations 2.19 and 2.20).

As with every correspondence system, in the visual maps that use them the rules by which marks are located and used as symbols only ever provide a parallel experience of the things they seek to map. First and foremost, they always display and exemplify the rules by which they are made. This does not make these drawings inaccurate. Rather, it simply points to the fact that this type of drawn map is concerned with generating a model that makes sense (and is useful) in its own terms.

Famously, Mercator's mapping system makes locations north of the equator appear larger than they are. Canada and Greenland appear to be many times larger than their real-world area whilst South

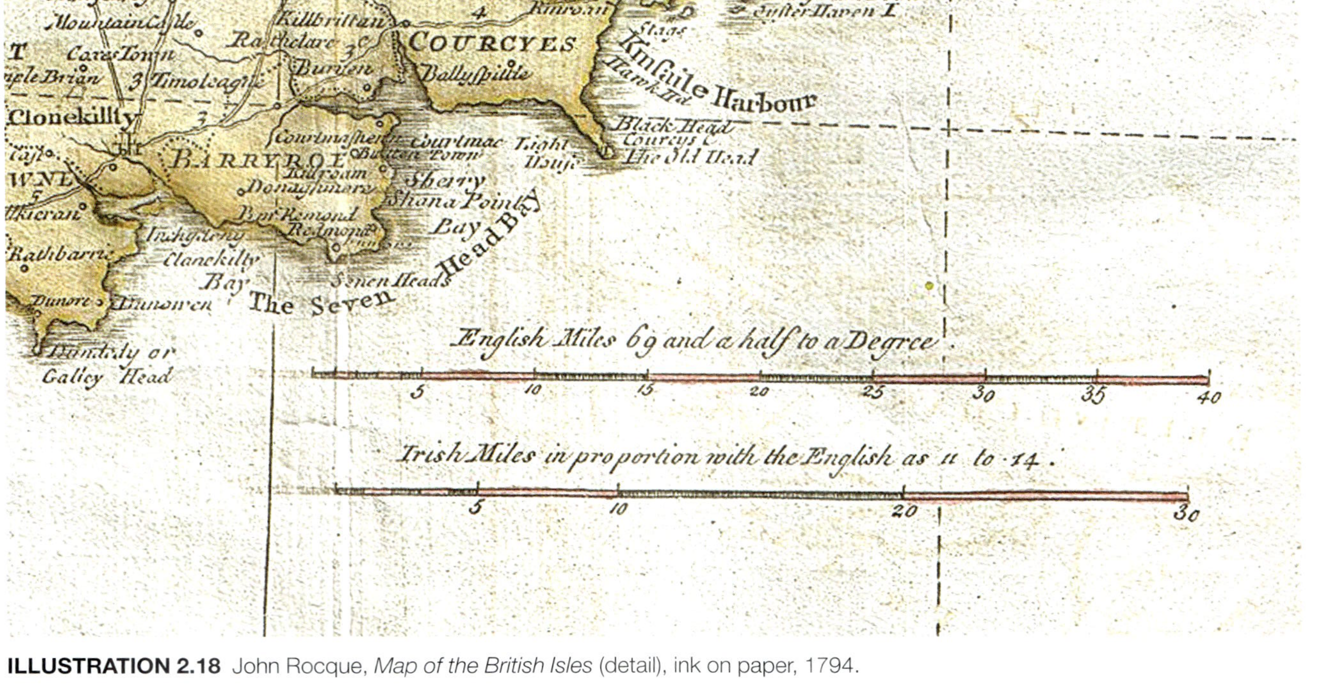

ILLUSTRATION 2.18 John Rocque, *Map of the British Isles* (detail), ink on paper, 1794.

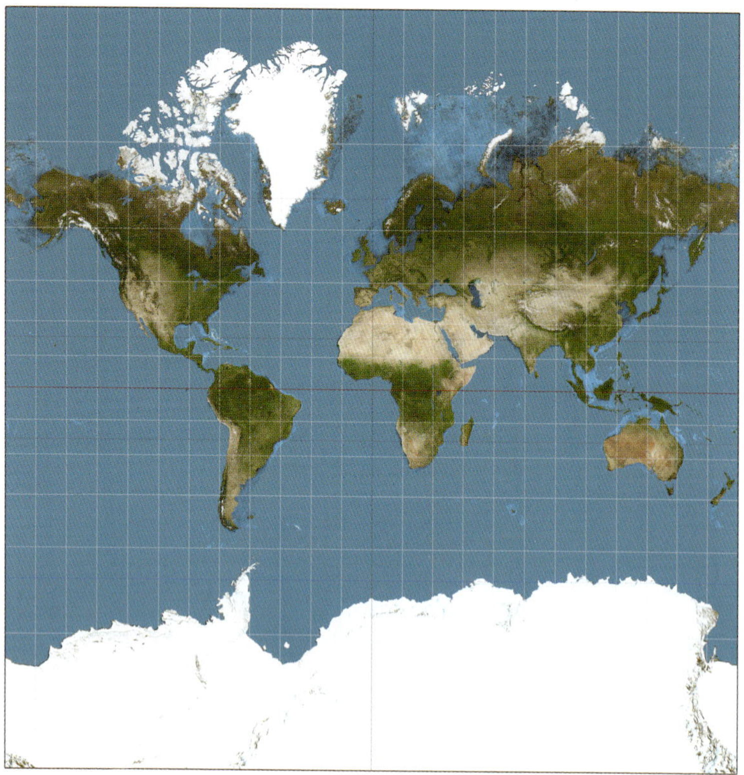

ILLUSTRATION 2.19 Daniel Strebe, *The World on Mercator Projection between 85°3′4″S and 85°3′4″N*, digital, 2011. Licensed under CC SA 3.0.

America appears much smaller. There is a political dimension to this characteristic. It has been claimed that the Mercator system promotes European, Russian and North American colonialism by visualizing the north as larger than the south, for example.

Hence, in the history of drawing systematic maps, there are a number of different correspondence systems, where each system produces a different type of representation. These representations inevitably contradict each other. For example, the Mercator system inflates the relative size of distances, the further from the drawn line of the global equator these distances are, distorting the representation of the sizes of land masses, whilst still conforming to the system. Alternatively, the Gall-Peters mapping system calculates the location of marks in a drawing

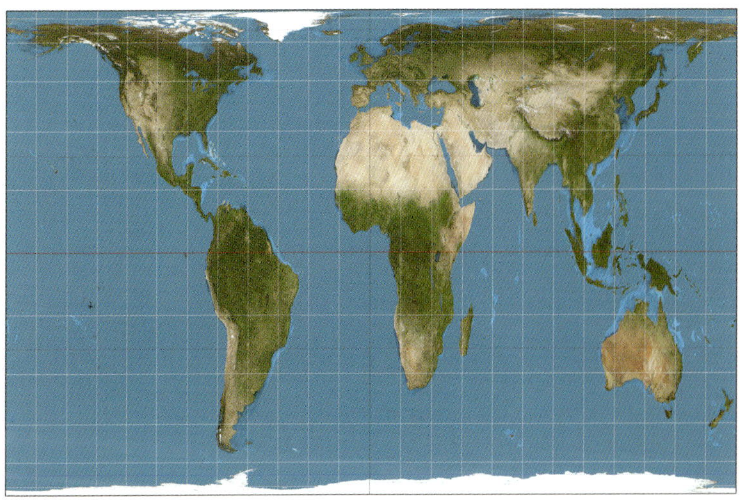

ILLUSTRATION 2.20 Daniel Strebe, *The world on Gall–Peters projection 15°graticule*, digital, 2011. Licensed under CC SA 3.0.

according to an 'equal area' system, in which the relative proportion of distances in the map derives simply from the relative proportion of distances between and within the things being mapped.

The aerial view currently used in most modern small-scale geographical maps, such as Ordnance Survey maps, imagines sight lines that establish the distances between features, seen from a height and also adopting an 'equal scale' method. In this system, the marked surface of the map is assumed to be an imaginary sea level. As a result, height and depth (nearer or further from the zero value of the surface sea level) are marked as numbers on contour lines. Systems like this build part of their correspondence between the drawing and its object on the idea that the sea level and the marked surface are a flat, infinite plane. They remain popular, because they reproduce the sense that the ground is flat. This is despite the fact that the data from which they are derived is collected by satellites capable of viewing not only the curvature of the earth but the entire globe from space.

Such systematic visualizations are not limited to geographic drawings. They encompass any type of external information, to which a systematic correspondence to locations and types of symbol on a drawn surface is made. Although less common than drawn geographic

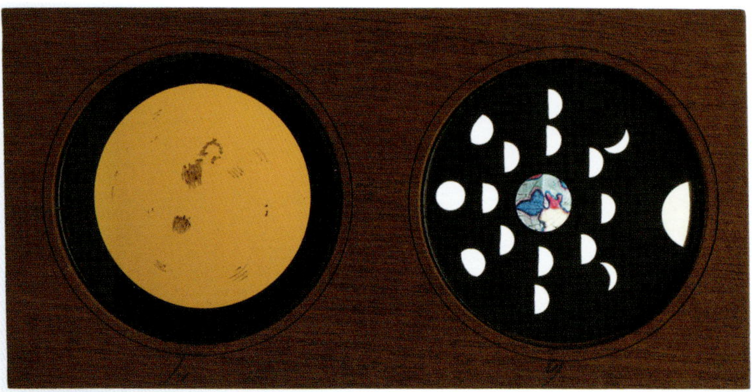

ILLUSTRATION 2.21 Lantern Slide, *Moon's Phases and the Sun*, 1847. Museums Victoria. Photograph by Jon Augier. Licensed under CC BY 4.0.

maps, weather systems, lunar phases and other types of relationships in time can also be mapped by systematic correspondence (Illustration 2.21). When this is done, maps segue immediately into visual metaphor and infographics, whilst always remaining drawings.

One of the earliest examples of this type of drawing shows a correspondence system that visibly represents the relationships between distance, duration, quantity and degrees of temperature. *The Russian Campaign of Napoleon*, drawn by Charles Minard and published in 1869, is considered to be one of the founding documents of interface studies because a number of distinct types of visual relationships, drawn on the page, have a mutual impact upon each other. As a result, the drawing is able to describe a much more complex situation than each of them could alone (Illustration 2.22). The drawing's legend, which describes the information that the map represents, says 'The graphic is notable for its representation in two dimensions of six types of data: the number of Napoleon's troops; distance; temperature; the latitude and longitude; direction of travel; and location relative to specific dates.'

The drawing of these different types of information creates an emotionally acute representation of a catastrophic event. Napoleon's army's' route towards Moscow and its subsequent retreat is represented by a corresponding line on the page, showing the distances covered. This line also shows the gradual decrease in the

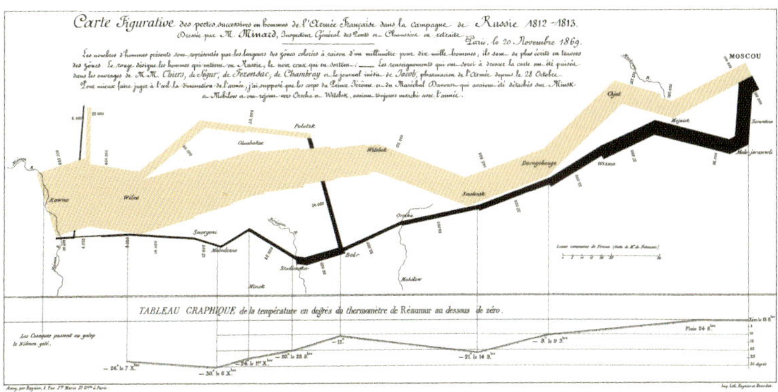

ILLUSTRATION 2.22 Charles Minard, *The Russian Campaign of Napoleon*, ink on paper, 1869.

number of troops, who had been killed through fighting, cold or disease as they progressed. The decrease in their number is represented by the decreasing thickness of the line. Returning to the Polish/Russian border, which is the army's starting point on the page, the line is thin, when compared with its extreme thickness at its origin. This comparison of thin and thick systematically represents the 500,000 deaths in the campaign, from the 600,000 outbound troops to the 100,000 troops who returned.

With a drawing that makes use of non-systematic correspondence relationships, symbolic meaning is found in the properties of items, such as colour and relative size and also categorical differences, ideas such as such as 'high', 'hot' or 'sacred', none of which require any systematic correspondence with relationships outside the drawing, to be meaningful. The so-called Ebstorf *Mappa Mundi* (1234) is a good example of the accumulation of a range of types of symbolic visual representation that are used without an encompassing system, in a single drawing (Illustration 2.23).

The drawing represents a world view, bringing together a combination of geographic items and religious ideas. Hence, Christ is shown enfolding the world, his head in the east (at the top of the map) and his feet in the west, with outstretched arms. Within his body, a geographic map has Jerusalem at its centre. In part, the real-world relationships between the items that are represented are determined by the relative location of symbols on the map's surface, but mostly

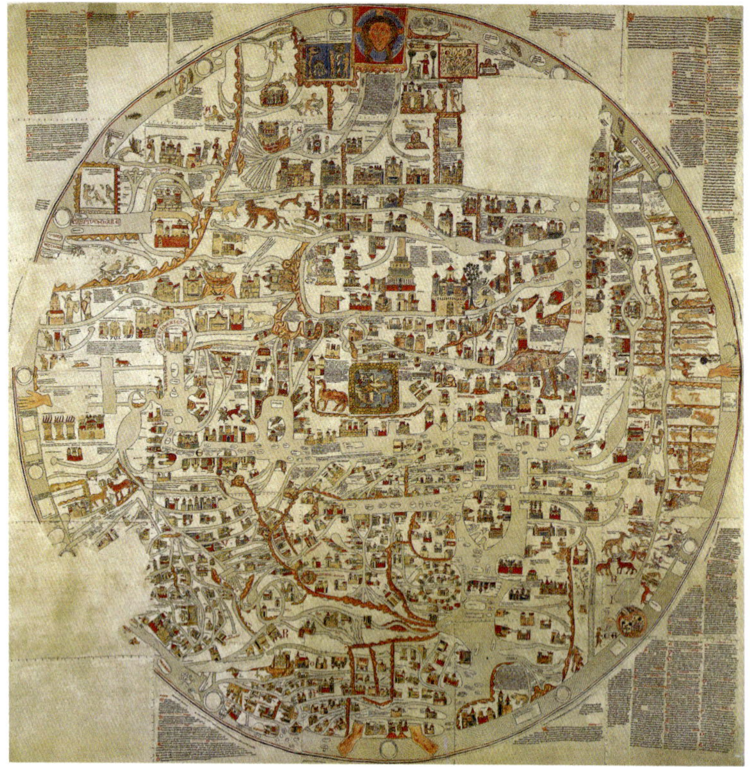

ILLUSTRATION 2.23 Gervase of Ebstorf, *Mappa Mundi,* paint and ink on vellum, 1234.

by their type. This accounts for the fact that, at first glance, the map might be mistaken for a practical orienteering guide. A drawing of a lion represents Rome, although Jerusalem is shown as a walled enclosure. The relative scale of symbols often derives from their relative religious significance, although, again, some symbols representing general geographic features are comparatively large, despite the fact that they are relatively insignificant, such as the drawing of a camel, which represents the Holy Land.

Non-systematic maps draw upon a range of types of existing knowledge, assumed on the part of their viewers, without which they don't make any sense. In the Ebstorf *Mappa Mundi*, without knowledge that the drawings of head, hands and feet are drawings of the idea of

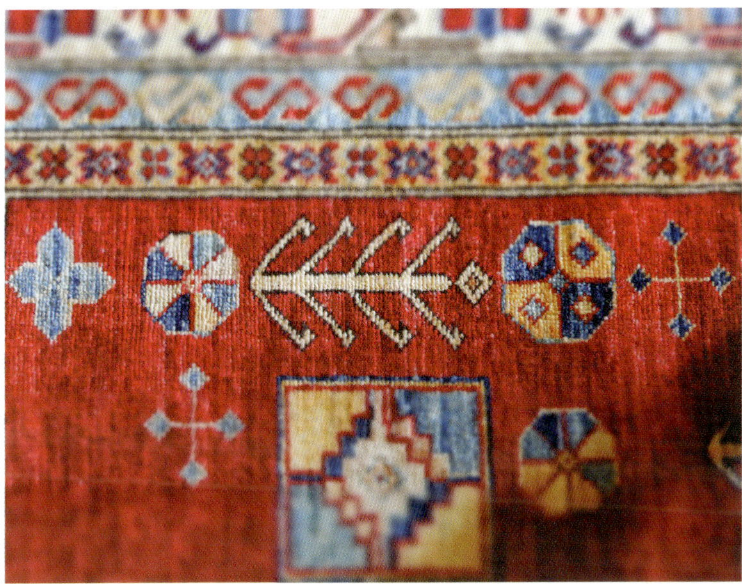

ILLUSTRATION 2.24 Anonymous, Caucasian rug, wool, 2014. Photograph by Gianni del Bufalo. Licensed under CC BY 2.0.

Christ's body encompassing the world, for example, these items are easily confused or even ludicrous. However, the existing knowledge needed to decipher the relationships in a non-systematic map does not perform the function of a 'key' to the symbols drawn in systematic maps because each item is variable in both appearance and function. Similar categories of existing knowledge also guide the distinction between Aboriginal Australian 'icons of country', which are drawings of time, space, history and story (which are used in ritual display), and drawings that are fundamentally plans for future actions and records of acquired knowledge. This extremely ancient tradition of drawing maps of whole ecologies thrives, exemplified in the unbroken tradition of Caucasian rug weaving, in which arrangements of shapes and colours map natural features of gardens or landscapes (Illustration 2.24), or the Kanpi artist Clarise Tunkin (b.1993).

Drawings can remain maps without mapping geographic features or the ideas about them, as Minard's military campaign map and Tunkin's work testifies. Any object, relationship or process can be visually mapped by drawing, even if these are imaginary.

Drawing systems representing three dimensions

Systematic correspondence systems, which govern the location of symbols in drawn maps, create different sight lines between drawn features. To understand these sight lines, the viewer of the drawing imagines that they are looking down at the ground from a specific height, for example. The ground is really 'ground zero' with maps because the marked surface represents sea level. It has zero value, as I have said, whereas any distance below this is a negative value and any distance above it is a positive value. However, the most famous systems for making systematic correspondences between distances in the real world and distances on the drawn surface imagine zero value as a vanishing point, beyond which nothing can be seen. These are spatial projection systems, also known as visual perspective systems.

A spatial projection system is a closed system of visual representation in which the location of marks on a two-dimensional surface systematically corresponds to the relative proximities between three-dimensional coordinates found in the viewed scene that is being represented. One of the most enduring of these systems was invented by architect Filippo Brunelleschi (1377–1446) and fully described in subsequent publications by architect and mathematician Leon Alberti (1404–1472) (Illustration 2.25). Such systematic equivalence of the

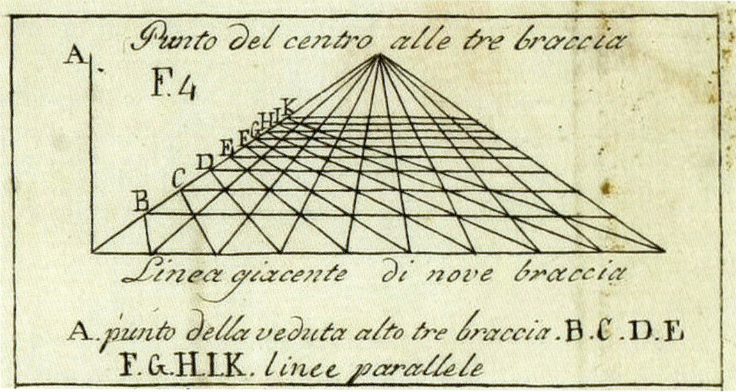

ILLUSTRATION 2.25 Leon Alberti, 'Vanishing Point', *De Pictura,* 1450 (1804 translation).

location of two-dimensional marks and three-dimensional coordinates governs all spatial projection systems, including those that calculate and produce the location of a horizon and horizon lines, vanishing points and points of view. As with systematic maps, the system governs the location of marks on the surface but not the shape of the marks themselves.

Typification

In spatial projection systems, the properties of marks and depicted objects are unimportant. It is their relative proximities to each other that are significant. Other ways of arranging marks on the page offer different choices to the drafter, which do not rely on spatial projection systems, in deciding upon the type and significance of the mark, beyond its location. For example, the survival of a tradition of observational drawing in the recording of archaeological evidence, in excavation, analysis and hypothesis, relies upon the fact that drawings represent only what the drafter considers to be relevant, in fulfilling the purpose of making the drawing. This selectiveness also facilitates the making of comparisons between drawings of different objects that have been drawn in the same way (Illustration 2.26).

The process of drawing selected, relevant features of a scene or object creates conventions in drawing style. These conventions show these selected features as typical. That is, similar features in a scene or object tend to be drawn in the same way. **typification** is also an efficient way of arranging visual information in drawings, because conventional marks are used to represent recognized aspects of a scene or object. To record typical features, a drafter is able to accumulate these marks without speculation or experiment. On the

TYPE Type is the identification of a subject, object or situation by applying knowledge of shared properties to specific instances. These properties are understood to be held in common, so that any subject, object or situation displaying these properties is also understood as belonging to the same type.

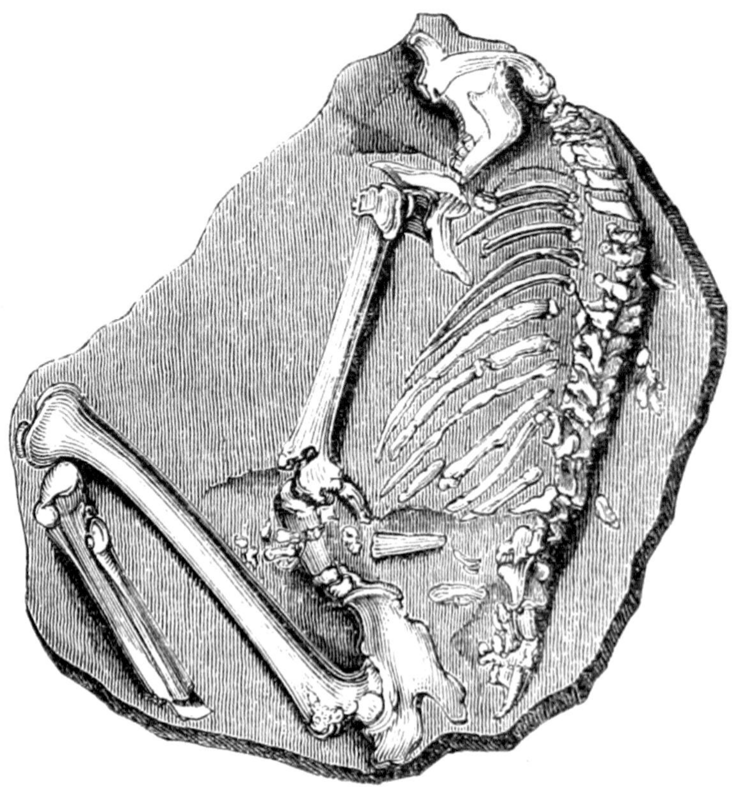

ILLUSTRATION 2.26 Gideon Algernon Mantell, *On the remains of Man and Works of Art Imbedded in Rocks and Strata*, wood engraving, 1850.

other hand, to photographically record the relevant aspects of a scene or object, a photographer has to exclude extraneous information in an editorial process. Photographs do not show selected, relevant aspects of a scene or object in a typical way. They always show every effect of light in a whole scene, at the moment when it hits a light-sensitive surface.

Archaeological drawings that are made by adopting this selective approach are undertaken exclusively to convey information – scientific disciplines might call it data – in answer to specific questions. For example, in recording an object of archaeological significance, the archaeologist might want to answer the questions: What was the

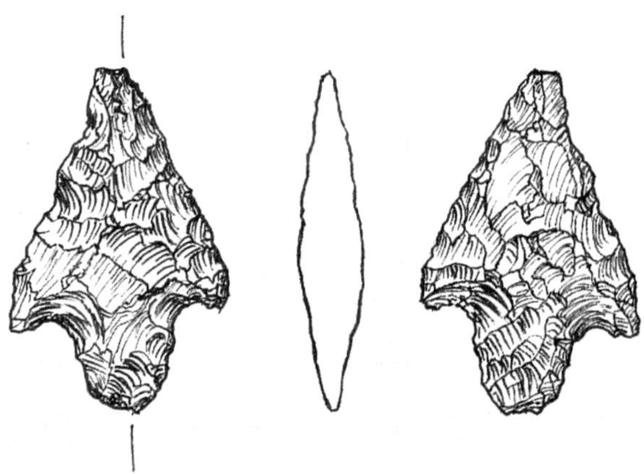

ILLUSTRATION 2.27 Anna Tyacke, *Drawing of a Barbed and Tanged Arrowhead*, ink on paper, 2005. Royal Institute of Cornwall. Licensed under CC BY-SA 2.0.

original purpose of the object? How was it made? What constraints on its making and its use were imposed by its material properties? To answer questions like these, archaeologists produce visual information by drawing in particular ways. As a result, stylistic conventions have arisen that help comparisons with drawings of other objects. Frequently, the object is drawn selectively from multiple points of view, to a strict scale, with a uniform thickness of line and the use of a range of types of marks, to represent different properties, such as stippling for texture or density or the use of a uniform degree of curved line to indicate types of manufacture of the object (Illustration 2.27).

This use of drawn symbols is, in itself, analytical. Symbols display the drafter's way of judging what is drawn. Just as a system-drawn map is drawn to provide information about the terrain it maps, it also provides information about the analytical skill of the drafter, who looked at the terrain to be mapped. Selective drawings tell the viewer that the drafter has analysed the object of their drawing, using subjective judgement to decide what a feature is, in the landscape, or what a feature of an object is. The great advantage of this type of drawing lies in the fact that it shows judgement. Archaeologists draw objects in order to make visible what they know, not only what can be seen.

Because selective drawing ignores some types of information in order to visually isolate and present other types, it is especially useful in presenting typical information or drawings of properties that are usually, if not always, found in objects. By and large, scientific instruments have been designed to represent particular instances and particular situations by recording material changes (such as temperature or weight) or traces (such as light, magnetism or radiation). Selective drawing, on the other hand, relies upon judgement, one of the advantages of which is the identification of types. Drawing remains a technique of scientific enquiry and record because science continues to require the representation of types as well as the objective representation of specific instances.

Writing

This selectivity, or the drawing of some features and not others, can be seen at the dawn of writing. Depictive drawings – those in which a viewer imagines that they experience themselves seeing a scene when they look at a marked surface – turned into writing when two things happened. First, drawings of specific scenes gave way to drawings of specific spoken words and parts of words, which represented those scenes. Second, the correspondence systems used to locate these words (that is, languages) were used to guide the location of marks on the surface. When these developments occurred, the proximity of these drawn marks was henceforward governed by the proximity of words in time, or the order and sequence of words arranged by a language. Further, because the shapes of the marks were relatively insignificant, beyond being recognizable and repeatable, drawn depictions of spoken scenes were edited by the selection of some features and not others, so that they were easier and quicker to draw again and again (Illustration 2.28).

Writing is defined by a single principle: time-based proximity relationships in a language system determine the visual proximity relationships of marks on a surface. In other words, the way in which a language arranges its constituent parts into words and sentences, over time, dictates the way in which the elements of writing are visibly arranged.

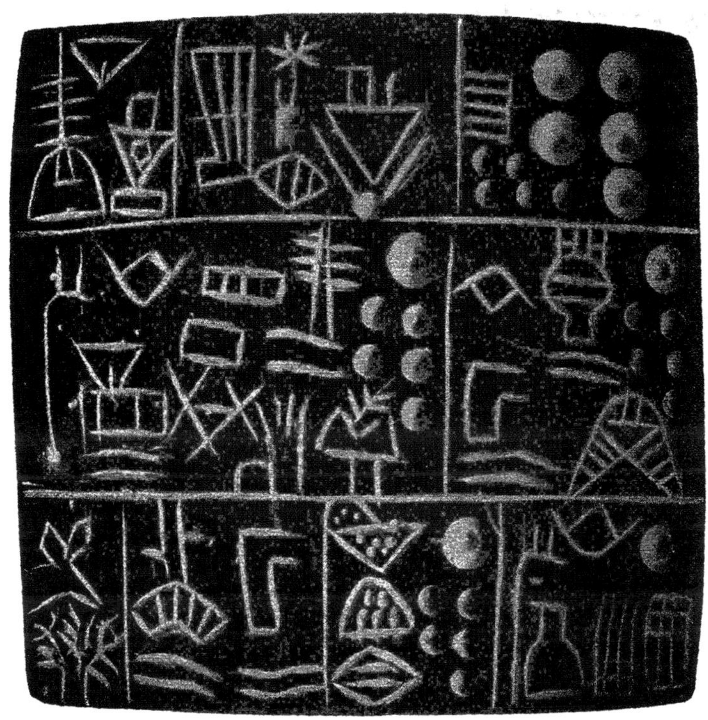

ILLUSTRATION 2.28 Anonymous, Archaic Cuneiform, clay, 3200 BCE.

However, two other things also influence the meaning of writing, although they do not define it: first, potential variations in the shapes of marks and, second, outside factors, or the circumstances in which writing is made and seen. Of themselves, written marks don't have any systematic significance. This idea might seem counterintuitive. Their inherent properties, such as their shape, colour, dimension or pattern, are only given significance, outside the system by habits of use. In this sense, writing resembles drawn three-dimensional projection systems, because both use the proximity of items in one system to locate the marks in the drawn system. For example, the yellow 'M' of the MacDonald's food chain is only seen as the letter 'M' because of its relationship to the word 'Macdonalds', whereas the yellow colour of the shape has brand associations that are not constrained by the name at all. In fact, a drawn mark that appears to be a letter, for example, cannot really be called a letter without being visibly located by a language system, even if it shares the properties of a letter.

This is the case even at a micro level. The basic building blocks of writing are called 'graphemes', that is, the parts of writing that cannot be divided any further. These have long been described according to their forms, as lines and dots. How much smaller can a drawn mark be than lines or dots? As with whole written letters, however, it is not the form of a mark (the line or dot) that makes a grapheme a grapheme. Rather, it is the mark's role in the system that is significant. The upstroke of the letter 'M' is only a basic building block of the letter when the whole 'M' takes its place in the writing system.

Writing also shares the ways in which its elements derive significance (that is, from a system of correspondences) with audible representations, such as speech and music. As a result, writing can be thought of as the visible notation of speech, in exactly the same way that musical scores are notations of other types of sound (Illustration 2.29). However, this has given rise to the idea that writing and musical notation differ,

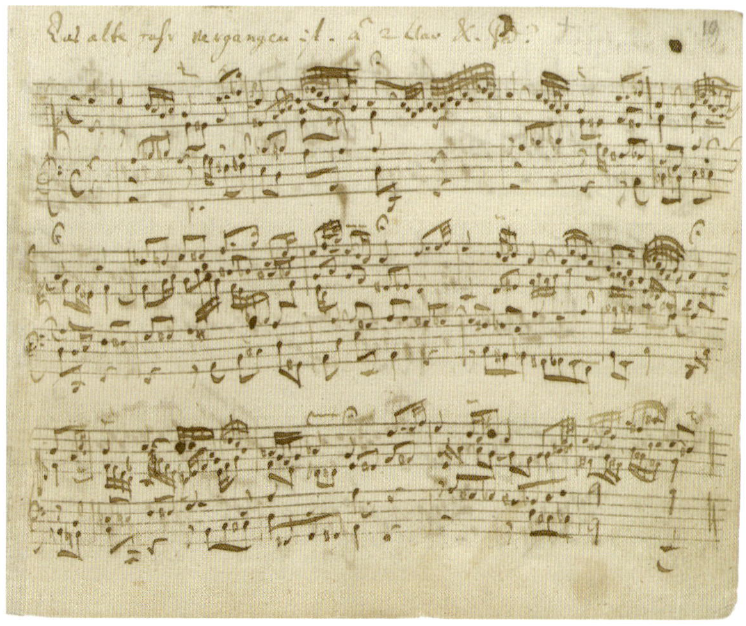

ILLUSTRATION 2.29 J. S. Bach, autograph manuscript of 'Das alte Jahre vergangen ist', ink on paper, 1720.

in that musical notation is always read as a plan that guides another activity (playing music that is guided by a notated score), whereas writing only produces the activity of reading what is written. There are obvious exceptions to this, such as written plays, which build the same relationships between the mark, reading and acting as musical notation builds between the mark, reading and playing, for example, or reading aloud.

Writing guides the visible placing of marks in relationship to each other, so that these relationships correspond to the relationships in an invisible language system. A language dictates systematic relationships of duration and rhythm, whereas writing reproduces these systems with distance and location. Writing produces spatial relationships, between marks on a surface, whereas the languages to which it corresponds produce temporal relationships. However, a significant characteristic is shared by both in the sequence of producing and receiving language in any medium (by making a mark or by speaking and by reading, viewing or listening). The activity of marking and the activity of reading creates not only the past and future of what is shown and seen, told and heard, but also establishes causes and consequences. The time-based relationships of language guide the spatial relationships of writing, affecting both content (what is said, written, heard or read) and the progress of how it is said, written, heard or read. This characteristic was self-evident to scribes in medieval Europe, who frequently described speaking, writing, drawing and reading as a journey.

Mark making across media

The omnipresence and variety of drawing is a result of the wide range of situations in which we think of the types of surface marking as drawing, when compared with other visual media. This variety mirrors the variety of purposes to which drawing has been turned. Drawing remains much more varied as a means of representation than any other medium, including digital media and superseding verbal media.

The reason for this is simple. Whatever else it is, drawing always turns out to be mark making, across media. The roots of the word in different languages indicate a wide range of ideas that mirror the wide range of circumstances in which a marked surface is representative. These roots announce the different traditions of drawings in language itself. For example, the English word 'draw' shares a root with 'drag', as distinct from the meaning 'to arrange' in French ('dessiner'). In draw and 'dessiner', we understand two different aspects of both the media and the circumstances of drawing: the activity of making the mark (in the word drag) and the activity of arranging marks (in the word 'dessiner').

In summary, a mark is any visual item that reproduces and represents the functional aspects of the system of representation from which it gains its meaning. These systems of representation include writing, mapping, any spatial projection, depictions and, ultimately, the conditions of the situation in which a mark is made and seen. In the sense that mark making defines drawing, the drawn mark cannot be identified outside a system of representation because it is the system that gives a mark its meaning. This is what distinguishes drawn marks from any other random mark that we might see.

The question for drafters is always 'What system do I use to guide me to place the mark?' The meaning of a mark usually derives either from its location, relative to other marks and to the rules that guide where the mark is placed (such as writing or spatial projection systems), or from the experience of visualization, or visual imagining.

In addition, marks only become meaningful if the representational system appears within a larger situation in which they are expected to provide a viewer with this experience, such as the trace of an action undertaken in the context of an art studio, using studio art techniques, where such activities are habitual, for example. No specific technology or set of social circumstances ever defines the mark (Illustrations 2.30–2.32).

Introducing the body

Every experience can be described in terms of the bodily resources that it employs. Hence, one group of experiences can be described in terms of another, according to the different ways in which these bodily resources are brought into focus. The experience of drawing a

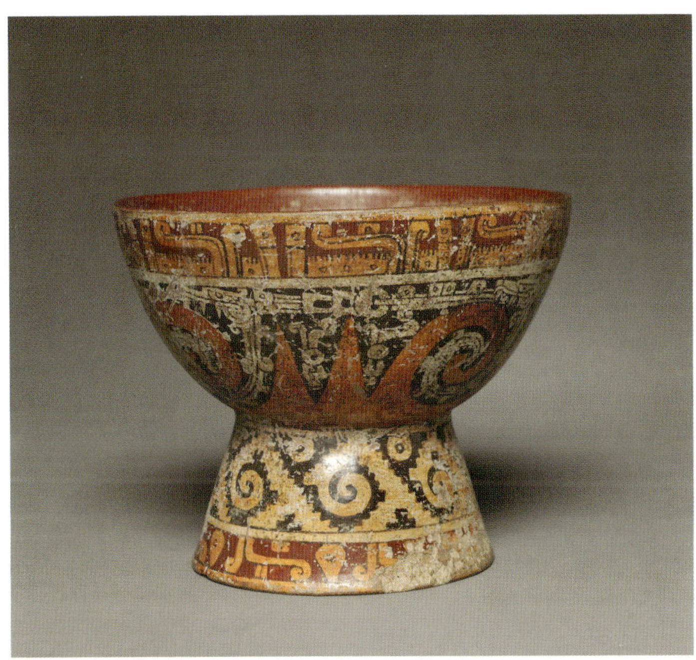

ILLUSTRATION 2.30 Anonymous, Mixteca-Puebla style pedestal bowl, Mexico, 900–1519. Cleveland Museum of Art.

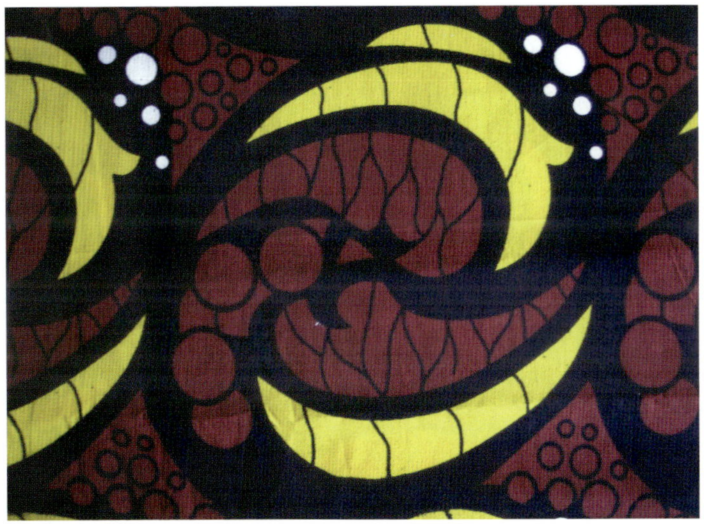

ILLUSTRATION 2.31 Anonymous, Kitenge print fabric, 2007. Photograph by Fanny Schertzer. Licensed under CC BY-SA 3.0.

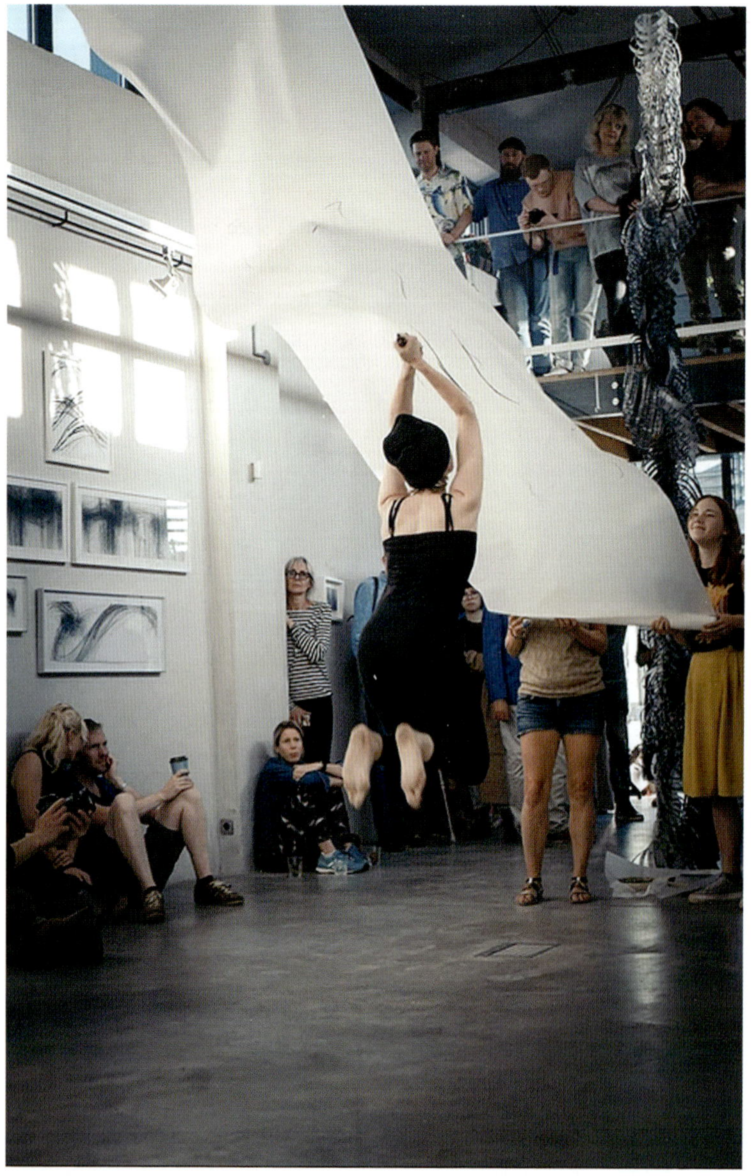

ILLUSTRATION 2.32 Jaanika Peerna, *Glacier Eligy (Tallinn)*, performance, 2018.

mark and the experience of viewing a mark share some of the same bodily resources. This allows comparisons to be made between shared experiences. It also allows translations to be made between them.

For example, the relative location of objects depicted as moving in space can be translated into the literal connections and disconnections between marks on a surface. Overlapping marks, clusters of marks, isolated marks and joined and interrupted marks all provide opportunities for imagining overlaps, groups, isolation, continuity and discontinuity between objects in a drawn scene. The sequence and rhythm of these connections and disconnections, which are made between marks on the surface, also provide literal translations of sequences and rhythms in the depicted scene. Perhaps the most obvious examples of the properties of drawn marks sharing the dynamic properties of the scenes that they depict can be found in comics. The directional marks of a comics 'speed lines' or staggered marks indicating a depicted movement are now so recognizable that they have come to characterize drawing itself, in the medium of comics (Illustration 2.33).

These translations and comparisons made between types of bodily experience, types of marks and the characteristics of depicted scenes, have prompted the idea that perception is a shared human capability. When it comes to drawing, some thinkers, including Philip Rawson (1924–1995), John Willats (1944–2006) and Patrick Maynard (b.1938), consider the human body to be, quite simply, a set of shared capabilities. This idea gives rise to one of the most significant and enduring approaches to describing drawing. It is still commonplace in studies of drawing, from practical 'how to draw' manuals through to theoretical work, to think about types of drawn mark as tools in a tool kit, which the drafter learns to recognize in existing drawings and to choose for a specific task, when they are making their own drawings.

According to Rawson, Willats and Maynard, specific types of mark are considered to be more suitable for specific drawing tasks. For example, marks that loop and connect to enclose an area on the surface of a drawing are thought of as the boundary of an object, distinct from its environment. It is identified as a shape. This boundary could be a silhouette or the boundary of a geographic enclosure on

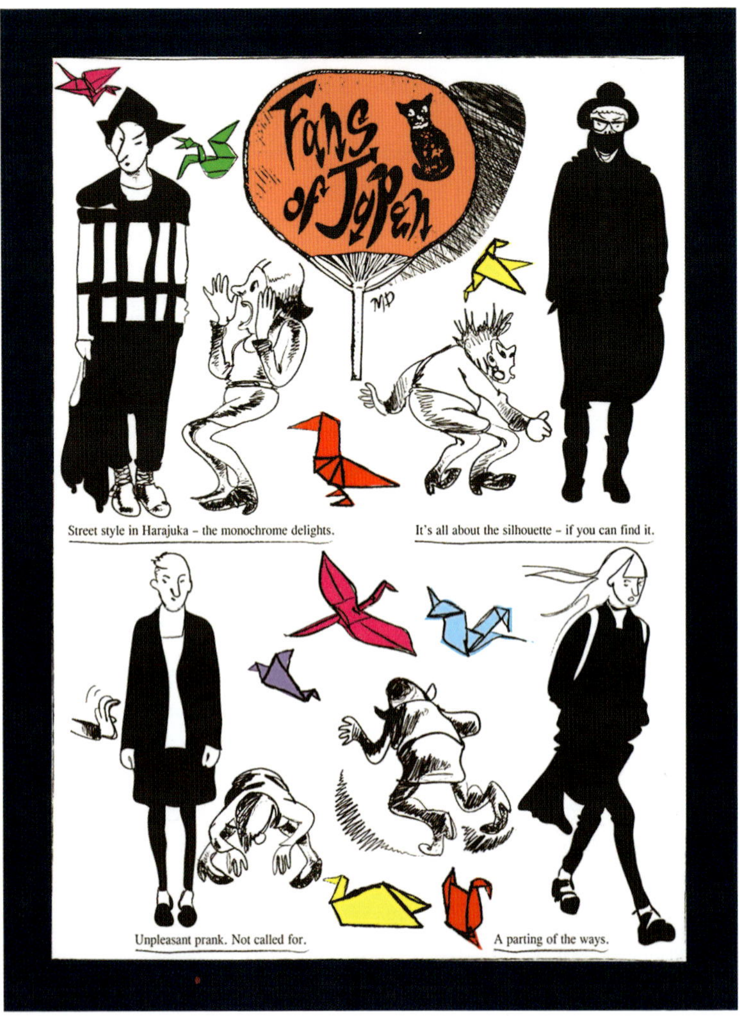

ILLUSTRATION 2.33 Simon Grennan, 'Fans of Japan', *Drawing in Drag by Marie Duval*, page 11, 2018.

a map. Whatever it represents, a mark with these characteristics is always thought to have two properties, inside and outside, according to this approach to drawing (Illustration 2.34).

This idea that types of drawn marks are tools in a tool kit is founded upon a simple assumption – the drafter selects from a range of possible

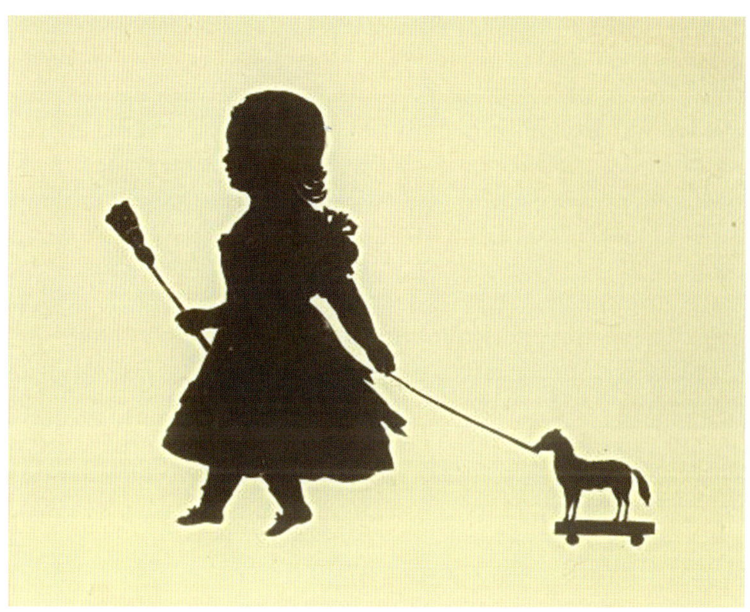

ILLUSTRATION 2.34 Anonymous, *Silhouette of Miss Jane Anne MacKenzie*, cut paper, 1830. Brooklyn Museum.

types of mark because human beings have a shared capacity to perceive these types of marks in the same way. If we take this approach to drawing and the body, drawing can also be seen as the history of drawing media. The similarities between marks used throughout this history are thought to provide enough evidence to generalize all experiences of drawing. Similar types of drawn marks are thought of as being perceived in similar ways.

In other words, this approach to drawing proposes that similarities between the bodies of the drafter and the viewer allow this to happen, despite other differences in people's experiences, such as gender, social status or history, for example. This idea claims that an ancient Egyptian perceived drawn marks in the same way as they were perceived by a Victorian actress, or as they are by a NASA astronaut, for example. In fact, the human body is more various than that. It isn't necessarily the case that ways of using and thinking about the opportunities and limitations offered by a drafter's body have been shared between different historical cultures or practitioners.

More recently, linguists interested in writing, such as James Martin (b.1950) and Paul Thibault (b.1953), have challenged this assumption about drawn marks. Rather than making up a tool kit, they propose that drawn marks are produced and guided by the drafter's attempt to achieve a goal, using the bodily resources at hand. Yes, these resources include types of drawing activities that might be similar to those that have been made before, but they specifically rely upon the particular aims, circumstances and broader bodily resources of the drafter, such as the weight, speed and scale of their body, plus ideas about these resources that guide the drafter according to their own experiences in specific places and at specific times. This idea allows for the appearance of entirely new types of marks and for identical marks to represent different things, for example. It also establishes the central significance of a specific relationship between the environment in which the drafter makes a drawing (including the goal of making a drawing and the ways in which the drawing is seen), the drafter's body and the materials with which the drawing is made.

3
TRACE

Before the twentieth century, it was more usual than not to describe drawing by referring to the relative capacities of different media, as we have seen. Even when drawing was described according to its different purposes, the drafter, the drafter's materials and the drafter's circumstances were bundled together with the drawing medium. Although the ideal visual imitation of the visible world demanded that the medium become invisible, the craft of making visual representations was organized by media – a printmaker was distinct from a painter and a painter was distinct from a technical drafter. These media and the skills required to manipulate them were well defined, even if some precocious drafters managed to master many media, most famously Leonardo da Vinci (1452–1519). This is how craft traditions and professional traditions emerge and are consolidated.

Following the Second World War, ideas about drawing shifted to consider the capacities of the drafter's body as much as the capacities of media. The idea that craft skills are always characterized by bodily resources might seem obvious. Before the middle of the twentieth century, this idea remained embedded in descriptions of the capacities of different media, but the body itself was overlooked. The focus on the characteristics of media, as the defining characteristics of drawing, simply encompassed this idea without recognizing it or scrutinizing it. In this view, the drafter's body was defined by the craft skills needed to manipulate media successfully rather than these craft skills being thought of as arising from the opportunities provided by the drafter's body.

The intuition that the characteristics of human bodies might guide or even dominate thoughts, including skills and intelligence, was revolutionary. It derived from a philosophical argument that sought to contradict a centuries-old idea that the human mind determines human identity. In contradiction to this, philosophers Edmund Husserl

(1859–1938) and Maurice Merleau-Ponty (1908–1961) proposed that the mobile, feeling body determined both consciousness and self-consciousness, encompassing both thought and perception. A shift in thinking took place in opposition to much broader, historic traditions of thought, which accorded higher status to the human capacity to think than to the capacities of a feeling and acting body, exemplified in the work of philosopher René Descartes (1596–1650).

As ideas of the significance of bodily experience took shape, drawing became a topic in debates about the body itself. On the one hand, thinkers such as Rosalind Krauss (b.1941) criticized technical traditions of drawing, such as the perspective grid, on the basis that three-dimensional projection systems act to control, restrain and limit the drafter's body. On the other hand, feminist thinkers, such as Simone de Beauvoir (1908–1986) and Andea Dworkin (1946–2005), criticized centuries-old traditions that considered the male body to be ideal. Critics of race, class and sexuality, such as Anne McClintock (b.1954), Franz Fanon (1925–1961), Sandra Bem (1944–2014) and Esther Newton (b.1940), proposed substantial revisions to ideas of the body in society. They criticized historic blindness to the differences between bodies, pointing to the richness of human experience, exemplified in contrasting conceptions of physical, emotional and social experiences of the body. Alfred Schütz (1899–1959) and Jack Douglas (b.1937) proposed that our bodies are revealed as part of a wider social environment rather than being self-bounded and individual.

The impact of these trends of thought upon ideas of drawing was significant. It established the ways in which the drafter's body encompasses and characterizes drawing media to become mutually productive. It was possible for a drawing to be a residue of a process, in which the fulfilling of the process dictates the form of the drawing. At the start of the twenty-first century, this idea had become a commonplace in fine art drawing. The idea allowed artists such as Margaret Roberts (b.1950) to create drawings like *Red Check* (2004). The drawing involved gallery visitors dancing, swinging, walking and running through a grid of red pigment placed by the artist on the floor (Illustration 3.1). The drawing mimicked older ideas of relationships between surface and marks, but turned a whole environment, prepared by Roberts, into an encompassing drawing that both transformed and recorded moving bodies.

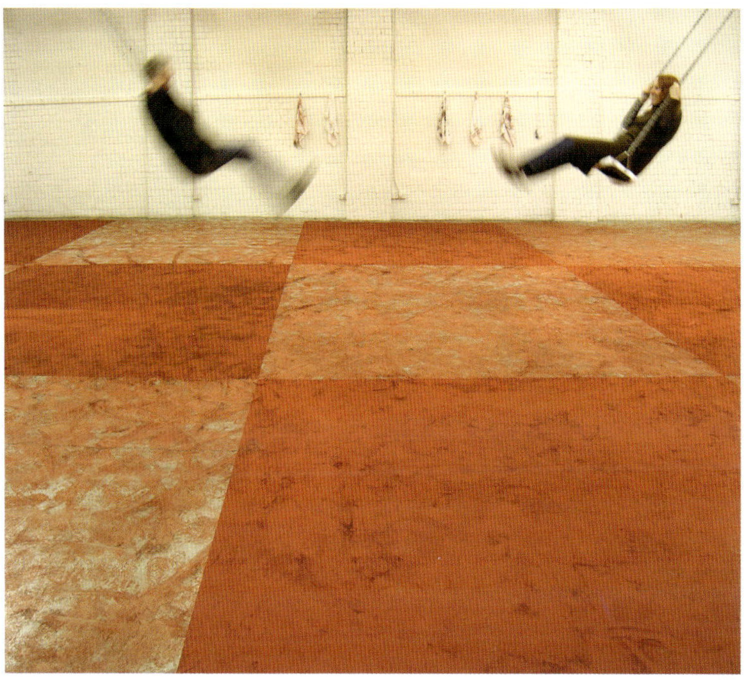

ILLUSTRATION 3.1 Margaret Roberts, *Red Check*, chalk, 2004. Photograph © 2004 Tony Warburton. Used with permission.

The surface

The idea that the environment encompasses both the drafter's body and drawing media reiterates one of the central choices facing drafter's and the viewers of drawings today: is the drawing surface a terrain to be travelled across, the boundary of some type of body, the visualization of an idea or a scene to be viewed – or some or all of these things at once? The history of drawn traces is also the history of the surfaces across, around, within or through which the trace appears.

The idea of the marked surface as terrain gives rise to a range of different conceptions of the actions made by the drafter's body. These are defined by the idea of the surface rather than by the characteristics of the drawn mark. Considered as terrain, the surface becomes an arena to be marked within, either along lines that are

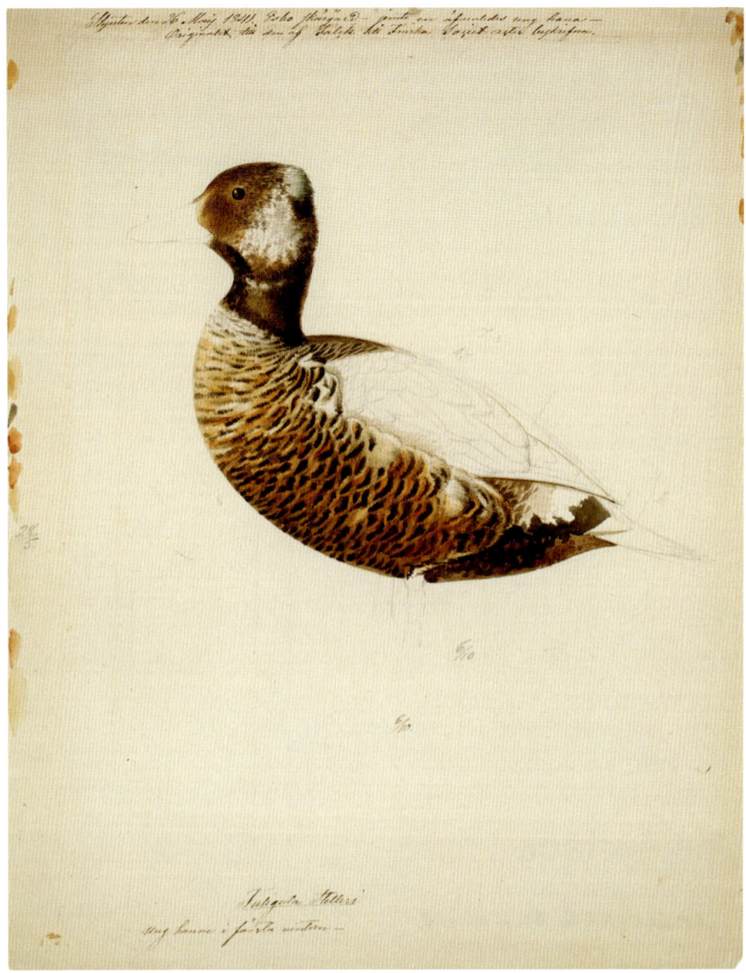

ILLUSTRATION 3.2 Magnus von Wright, *Stellar's Eider, Young Male* (unfinished), pencil and watercolour on paper, undated.

imagined as they are traced or across the surface, between imagined locations. The former way of imagining the movement of the drafter, on the surface as terrain, is characteristically mobile. It imagines the drawn image as a network of traces of past journeys that are always incomplete. There is always a move (and a mark) that is yet to be made (Illustration 3.2). On the other hand, the latter way of imagining the drawing surface identifies destinations. These destinations are established, connected and consolidated as the marking line reaches them and stops. However, a surface upon which a mark draws itself along, brings itself spontaneously into being. Alternatively, a mark that aims to connect two imagined locations makes tangible an already imagined world.

The surface of the drawing as the skin of a body

The idea of the marked surface as the skin of a body produces experiences of the widest range of differences of pressure and resistance to pressure. The pressure of air on the marked surface makes a comparison with the pressure of air on the drafter's body, giving rise to sensations of comparative softness (less resistance to pressure) and hardness (more resistance to pressure) and of temperature (cooler or hotter), moisture (dryer or wetter) and texture (rougher or smoother). Artist Andy Goldsworthy (b.1956) has explored the idea of the drawing's surface as a skin. In the 1990s, Goldsworthy collected snow from locations in Scotland and placed it on sheets of paper, to melt and dry. The consequent marks provide a detailed visual record of the snow's constituent parts, literally laying them open to view. These snow drawings visually reproduce the relationship between the earth's surface and the marked surface as a skin, over which the atmosphere of particular parts of the country are made permanently visible in the drawing.

Considered as skin, the marked surface is not a threshold to be crossed but the boundary of the drawing that is physically nearest to the drafter, which the drafter reaches out to meet, when a mark is made. The variety of types of meeting between the body of the drawing and the drafter's body is evidenced in the wide variety of words describing the possible physical and emotional characteristics of this meeting: touch, press, kiss, brush, pinch, stroke, bruise, push, tickle, slap, punch, hit, pummel or knead, for example. These verbs for physical contact and transformation are also used to describe the characteristics of the variety of ways of making a drawn mark.

The surface as a visualization of an idea

Neither this materalization of the surface, considered as a skin, nor the idea of a drawing revealing itself as terrain (through path-finding) encompasses the possibilities of considering the surface as the visualization of an idea. The concept of the surface as the visualization of an idea pops up in surprising and unexpected places. For example, to understand an artist's self-portrait drawing, both artist and viewers need to imagine that the surface of the drawing is a view of a mirror, in which the drafter has seen themselves at some moment in the past. This idea is a curious variation on the idea that the marked surface is invisible. As we have seen, depictive drawings sometimes make use of formal spatial projection systems to guide the location of marks on the surface and present a measured scene to view. These systems help viewers to imagine that the marked surface is invisible, so that the depicted scene can be viewed as if through a window. With self-portraits, this scene relies upon the idea that the surface is a reflection of a scene in a mirror.

In a completely different example of the surface of a drawing being thought of as an idea, the leaves of a month-to-view calendar rely upon the idea that every event for the duration of a month is encompassed by the surface of the page and that this surface duration exactly reproduces other leaves, encompassing the duration of events over a period of a year.

The limits of the drawing

The concept of the surface as an idea neatly underpins related approaches to thinking about the mark. If depictions require the viewer to imagine that the marked surface is invisible, then the furthest extent of the surface, often described somewhat misleadingly as an edge, takes on particular significance. The edge is imagined to be the frame of an opening, or window, through which the drawn world is seen. In Western traditions of depiction, this frame does not dictate the geometry of the imagined scene, viewed through the imagined window. Rather, the point from which the scene is viewed, through the window, governs the imagined arrangement of the depicted scene beyond. The shape and size of the window itself is irrelevant.

In other drawing traditions, the edge of the surface is thought of quite differently. For example, in Eastern traditions of drawing, the edge of a surface and its shape influence the first mark that the drafter makes. This is categorically different to Western traditions of thinking about the edge as a window or threshold. In Eastern traditions, the edge of a piece of paper is a trace of the activity of selecting and removing the potential drawing surface from the rest of the world. According to this approach, the edge is a visible component of the drawing (Illustration 3.3).

This tradition of approaching the surface is founded upon an understanding of the enfolding ecology in which drawings are made. For Chinese drafters, from the Han Dynasty (206 BCE–229 CE) onwards, drawing has been thought of as an activity that makes the mind and senses visible, selecting specific ideas and sensations from a total ecology by paying attention to some things and not to others. Although this approach should not be confused with the idea that these drafters were selecting items from a menu of experiences, the act of paying attention rather brings what is thought or felt to the forefront, making it available

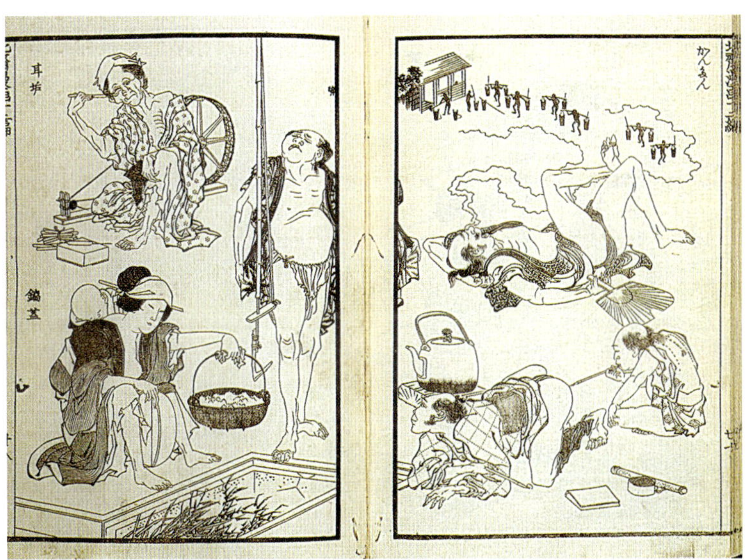

ILLUSTRATION 3.3 Katsushika Hokusai, *Manga XII*, woodblock print, 1834.

for scrutiny. This bringing to the fore is exemplified by the surface and its extent, or the surface's edge, before the drafter even makes a mark.

The significance of drawing media

Ideas about the material properties of the surface, on which a drawing is made, can also be significant. We often talk about the craft skills that a drafter gains, to manipulate drawing media, in terms of the properties of the media themselves. We can judge the level of a drafter's skills, in making use of a pencil, pen, brush or ink by their ability to control the properties of the materials. I might be skilful at drawing with a pencil but not so skilful at drawing with ink, for example. The properties of the media are different and the skills I need to manipulate them are different.

There is often an established terminology for these media properties. Think of the differences between a pencil marked 'H' (hard) and one marked 'B' (soft), for example. These terms are located on the graphite grading scale because graphite is the material that makes the mark when we use a pencil. The scale runs from '9H' (hardest), which produces the palest graphite mark, to '9xxB' (softest), which produces the darkest graphite mark. Paper made for drawing also has a range of terms to describe different properties, according to how and where it is made.

To some extent, then, when we describe the properties of drawing media – materials and surfaces – we also describe the skills that the drafter has to acquire, to make use of them. If we describe a drafter's brush as 'loaded' with ink, we are also describing the possibilities open to the drafter for making a type of mark. In contemporary Chinese drawing traditions, for example, there are specific terms for these possibilities. 'Shui-pi' (water brush) and 'kan-pi' (dry brush) are both descriptions of the properties of media, types of skills and the types of drawings that can be made. Earlier Chinese traditions, from the Qing period (1644–1912), also brought these things together as combined ideas, such as 'ts'un' (hemp-fibre) marks or 'tsa-pi' (rubbed-brush) marks (Illustration 3.4). Western traditions of drawing have not really developed an equivalent vocabulary for specific characteristics that bind together media, skill and the drafter's body in a single description, although the grading of graphite pencils provides one example of a substitution of one characteristic for another (such as 'soft' for 'dark').

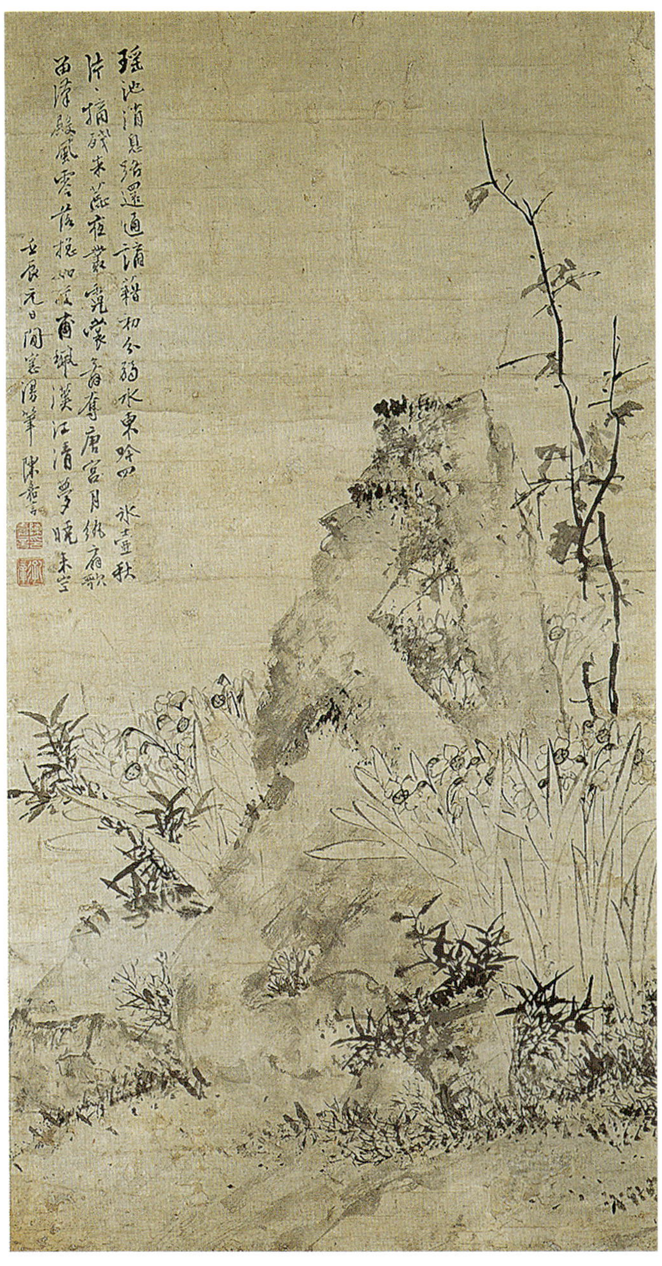

ILLUSTRATION 3.4 Chen Jaiyen, *Bamboo, Rock and Narcissus*, ink on paper, 1652.

Trace, media and body

Today, however, it is not such a large step for Western drafters to understand that descriptions of media properties and craft skills also describe ideas about the capabilities of the drafter's body. It follows that the properties of the mark trace the properties of the body making the mark. For example, the historic focus on the drafter's hand has always implied a range of possible postures and gestures that the body has to make to produce a drawing. The size, shape and texture of handheld drawing materials and surfaces have generated long-standing habits of drawing, which involve these postures and gestures. For example, the drafter views the drawing's surface at arm's length because arm's length is an imposed (though not conclusive) distance between the hand and the drafter's eyes.

Physical and environmental constraints such as these are still explicitly described in manuals that teach drawing. The student is instructed to sit and to hold drawing materials in specific ways. These are understood to make the manipulation of drawing materials easier. They are instructions that help the drafter to control their own body prior to manipulating the materials themselves. In the earliest Western drawing manuals, instructions of this type are often pages long. In Butler Williams's (18?–18?) popular *A Manual for Teaching Model-Drawing from Solid Forms*, published in 1843, precise instructions for the posture and position of the drafter's body run to fourteen pages.

This model of a drawing environment, which is characterized by the drafter's body, is still reproduced by the development and production of drawing materials with particular properties (such as 'hand-held') and the habitual ways in which drafters make use of them. We have all made a mark with a biro on a piece of paper lying on a table. To do this, we have positioned our bodies relative to the pen, paper and table and made gestures within these constraints to draw our mark.

Some drawing traditions have always contradicted these habits of media, gesture, reach and environment. In particular, the long, continuing traditions of Polynesian sand drawings (Illustration 3.5), Australian Aboriginal peoples' land drawings, the Nazca people's trench drawings of the first century BCE and the chalk hill drawings of Bronze Age Europeans (1000–700 BCE) (Illustration 3.6). The drawing media

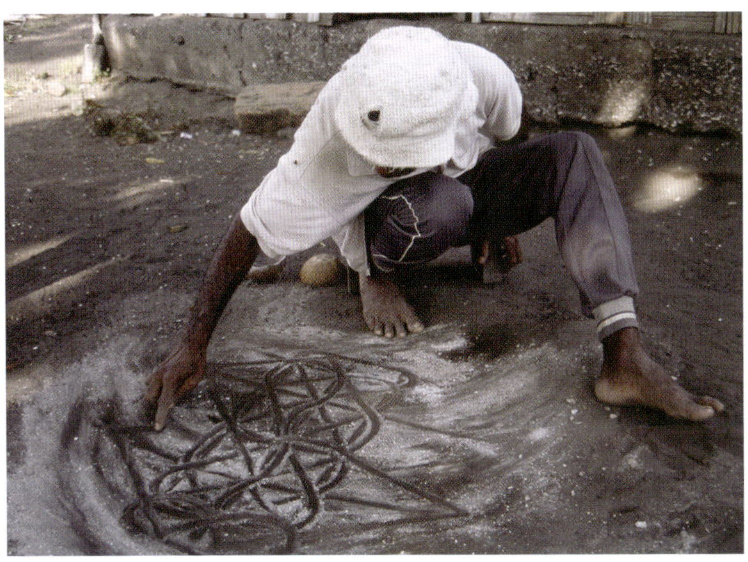

ILLUSTRATION 3.5 Stephen Zagala, *John Teungkon drawing a sand drawing, Craig Cove*, 1999.

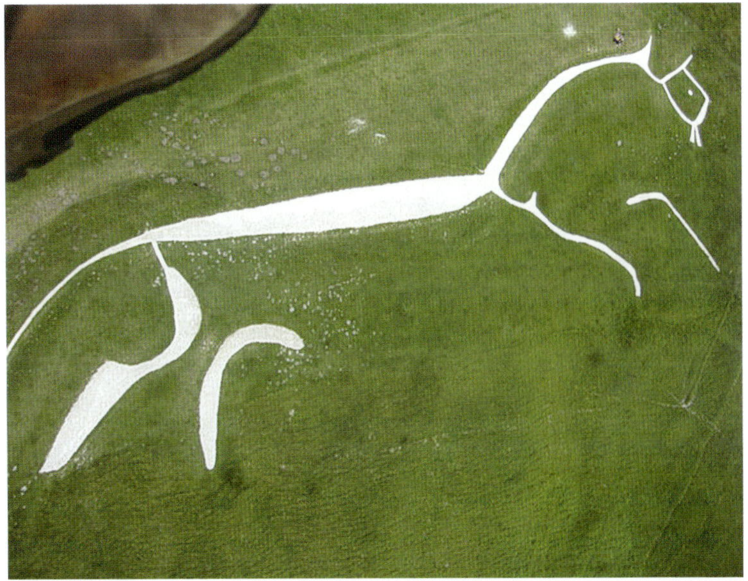

ILLUSTRATION 3.6 Uffington White Horse, cut turf, 1000–700 BCE. Photograph by Dave Price. Licensed under CC BY-SA 2.0.

underpinning these traditions demanded bodily resources, postures and gestures that are very different to the bodily resources involved in making a drawing with a pen on a piece of paper. As a result, drawings in these traditions produce very different conceptions, representations and traces of the drafters' bodies. Indeed, these drawing traditions are often collaborative, involving multiple drafters working together on a distributed task that would have been impossible for a single drafter alone. As a result, these collaborations leave traces that transform the individual drafter's body.

Throughout the 1950s and 1960s, artists and drafters started to reconsider the implications of the ways in which drawn traces define and represent experiences of the drafter's body. Drafters redefined drawing according to the widest range of experiments with their bodies. For example, artist Richard Long (b.1945) considers the marks he makes by walking different paths, in different ways, to be drawings. Carpet weavers manipulate a wide range of threads in a wide range of ways, such as twisting, folding, winding, tangling and untangling. The traces of these activities are drawings (Illustration 3.7).

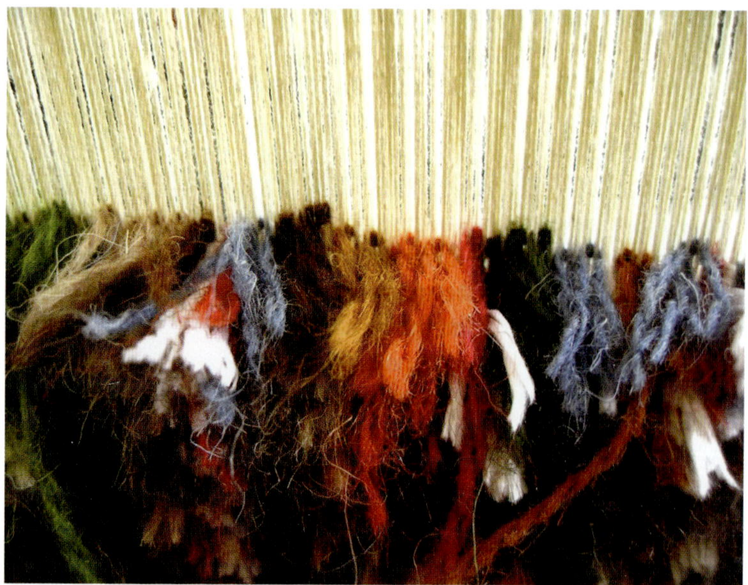

ILLUSTRATION 3.7 Carpet weaving in Mahan, Iran, 2007. Photograph by Fulvio Spada. Licensed under CC BY-SA 2.0.

Trace and style

The body was always present in drawings as defined by media. The body is found in the earliest discussions of artistic style, or the representation of the individual traits of a particular drafter or artist in the way in which they fulfil their craft. A unique style of production has always been thought of as a personal signature and, as such, has been considered as an unmediated means of experiencing the individual traits of the maker.

This idea has been applied largely to the task of recognizing the unique style of a particular artist in their drawn traces. The ability to distinguish between unique drawing styles is called connoisseurship. Although hardly a science, the methods that have been developed to enable connoisseurs to identify drafters are complex. They are founded on the connoisseur's great familiarity with all of a drafter's work and the resulting ability to make comparisons and recognize differences between different traces.

However, the significance of the ways in which drafter's make use of drawing media has, from the twentieth century, led to self-conscious deskilling. Although not exactly contradicted by connoisseurship, modern artists in particular have adopted the appearance of naivety in the ways that they use drawing media. They were motivated by a desire to not let draft skills confuse or obscure the directness of their expression, in the drawn traces made by their bodies. Drafters have used methods of 'blind' drawing (literally drawing whilst blindfolded) and 'other handed' drawing, in which the drafter uses their least customary hand to make a drawing. If they are right handed, they use their left. Both of these methods of trying to reach 'uncultured' expression were pioneered by artists Robert Rauschenberg (1925–2008) and Cy Twombly (1928–2011) in the 1970s.

The desire to strip individual bodily expression of a veneer of culture has much in common with the idea that a drafter's style is a unique and individual signature. Both ideas assume that we have a fundamentally unreasonable, subconscious mind, as distinct from our reason and consciousness. According to this idea, the subconscious mind refuses control or constraint and only reveals itself when learned rules are put aside, broken or overturned. Accordingly, this revealed 'self' is the authentic self. Hence, the drafter's individual style is thought of as revealing their individual characteristics. Both 'blind' and 'other handed' drawing are methods for overturning the craft conventions that obscure the drafter's unique personality.

Perhaps the most famous and enduring of these techniques is the method of 'automatic' drawing, in which the drafter attempts to lose control of their hands and the media they are manipulating, to make marks at random. This technique is associated with both psychoanalysis and with spiritualism, both of which continue to make use of it to reveal invisible or supernatural forces. In psychoanalysis, these forces are the emotional forces of the subconscious. In spiritualism, they are ghosts of the dead (Illustration 3.8).

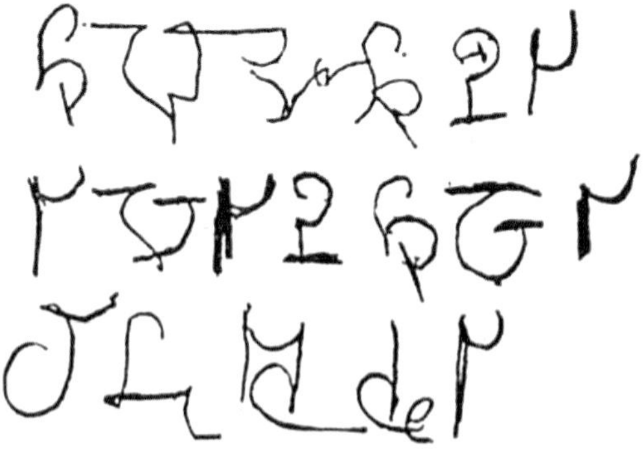

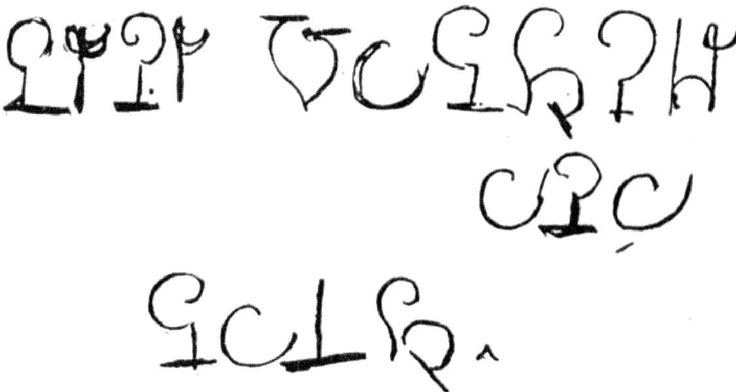

ILLUSTRATION 3.8 Hélène Smith, *Martian writing*, ink on paper, 1897.

Trace as evidence

Whatever other function the mark might have, drawn marks always record the ways in which they are made. This record does not find its origin in the characteristics of any medium, but rather in the characteristics of the drafter's body. The mark that records the way in which it is made finds significance in its physical origin. The drawn mark is always a **sign** of the activity of its production. Its significance lies in pointing to the origin of its own making, in the actions of the drafter's body. The philosopher Charles Peirce (1839–1914) called this type of mark an 'indexical sign', in other words a visual representation that points to the way in which it made, as if with an 'index' ('pointing') finger.

> **SIGN** A sign is a representation or any entity that indicates the presence of something else. Within this broad definition, the tradition of semiotics (thinking about and explaining signs) identifies three ways in which signs function to represent other things: first, by making a physical connection between the sign and what it signifies; second, by having the sign resemble what it signifies; and, third, by using a learned set of conventions that dictate that the sign means something, that it is agreed that 'this' means 'that'.

Peirce's description establishes the capacities of the drafter's body as foundational for drawing. The description also applies to every drawing, regardless of the medium in which it is made. This might sound counterintuitive. What of those mark-making media that interpose multiple boundaries between the drafter and the mark, such as digital drawing media? In fact, these media still **index** the activities of the drafter's body, but in ways that are widely different from each other.

> **INDEX** In drawing, a mark is always an indexical sign of the activity of its production. It signifies, in part, by indicating a physical connection with its object.

In fact, these media index diverse bodies. As a result, these media often baffle ideas of authorship that are based on the idea of a single author because diverse authors (and authors' bodies) are indexed in their digital programmes and the windows for individual action that these digital programmes are created to provide.

As an index of a body, a drawn mark has causes and offers consequences. These causes and consequences are always visible, despite the fact that some drawing technology is designed specifically to obscure them. As viewers, we might not understand the activities that cause a drawn mark because we lack knowledge of technical processes (such as the ways in which keyboards, computer chips or printing machines are made) or lack knowledge of the social relationships involved in its production (such as the vast numbers of collaborators fulfilling different roles in the production of an animated movie). In these cases, every marked trace still provides visible evidence of its causes, but we do not understand what we see. As viewers, the consequences of the mark are easier to determine or, at least, are easier to understand. The viewer's experience of a drawing is always a consequence of the drawing.

In addition, there is a distinction between marks that trace the activities of the drafter's body and activities that index the drafter's body. Traces are the direct remnants of drawing activities. Traces index, or point to, the activity of the body from which they originate, but they also leave remnants. Trace is a subset of index.

This distinction is particularly significant relative to descriptions of different mark-making activities and descriptions of different technical processes. Digital drawing technology can index activities of the body without tracing them (that is, without producing direct remnants), whereas a mark made in the sand with a finger is always both an index and a trace.

Movement, mind and absence

Drawn traces are frequently considered to be signs of movement. Even though active movements make a drawing, it is still. Hence there is a direct relationship between different types of movement and the different types of marks that they trace. The mark is a visible sign of the activity that made it. If you make a big movement, you make a big mark. With some media, if the drafter presses harder, the mark gets darker. If the drafter moves quickly, the mark looks spontaneous.

This relationship has also been thought of as providing evidence of the mind of the drafter. The argument goes that the mark traces the movement and the movement is motivated by an idea in the drafter's mind. If this is the case, then the mark also traces the idea. This way of thinking, which was introduced by philosopher Henri Bergson (1859–1941), proposes that being and thinking happen as a single event. The mark that traces the body's movement is a sign for the progress of the whole thinking and feeling body and not only the physical body.

The flip side to this conception of trace proposes that it is experiences of the body that produce the mind. These experiences of the body act to direct ideas and to make them meaningful rather then the other way around. Since the 1970s, drafters have used this idea to explain how visual representations work according to a 'body ecology'. Rather than revealing a mind in a body, drawn traces form part of comprehensive feedback loops and reciprocal relationships. These create a structure in which both physical and cognitive experiences build with each other to become significant.

This approach underpins the work of artist Rebecca Horn (b.1944), who demonstrates the connections that characterize the tracing body by building elaborate physical prostheses with which to draw. By changing her body capacities, through the addition of physical 'additions', she aims to discover changes in the types of actions and marks that she can make. In Horn's opinion every drawing technology, including the finger in the sand and the humble piece of chalk, is a modification and reformation of the body. It is an addition to the body. But Horn thinks that these reformations do not provide evidence of a mind in the body but, rather, show how specific types of bodies are connected to and disconnected from different environments and different ideas.

Not all drafters accept this. The concept that the drawn mark is a trace of the actions and thoughts of the drafter has now reached such a level of sophistication that it even encompasses ideas about the absence of marks! These absent marks act as invisible rhythmic punctuation. The idea is paradoxical, because the marks are absent. The edge of consciousness, silence and stillness is thought to be traced by this absence.

A precursor of this way of thinking about trace is the drawing *Erased de Kooning Drawing* (1953) by artist Robert Rauschenberg (1925–2008), made by rubbing out a drawing by the artist Willem de Kooning (1904–1997). A lot has been written, in negative terms, about Rauschenberg's drawing as though it removed de Kooning's drawing. However, the drawing still exists, so the erasure can also be thought of as accumulation. The activity of erasing the marks adds to the drawing. By erasing de Kooning's marks, Rauschenberg effectively created his own. He was making another mark rather than taking a mark away. The idea of erasure as removal is a very firmly lodged one, but the fact is that erasures are really types of marks. They differ from other types of marks by representing removal. Erased marks have a unique place in thinking about trace, because erased marks are marks that both over-draw other marks and signal the absence of a mark at the same time.

These complex approaches to discussing the drawn traces of the body have been inspired by thinking about moving image media, such as film, video and digital video. Although moving images are frequently depictions (although not always), the sequences of different still images create a true illusion of movement in the depicted scene, which viewers imagine themselves seeing. Slight changes between the 'frames' of a film, or changes between the patterns of pixels on a digital screen, create the illusion of the movement in the depiction. This relationship has been described as the defining relationship in moving image media. Art historian Edward Krčma (b.1977) has outlined the transformation of static elements into experiences of change and duration, with all the metaphorical sense of fragmentation, dispersal – and even absence – that this implies. Looking at a series of drawings by Henri Matisse (1869–1954), Krčma describes how this idea of moving images redirects the experience of Matisse's drawing sequence, *Themes and Variations* (1941–1942), towards duration, which is achieved through repetition and incremental change.

Choreographing traces

This development of ideas about trace emerged in the late 1960s and was also prompted by drafters who brought concepts from the performing arts to bear upon drawing. In particular, performer Trisha

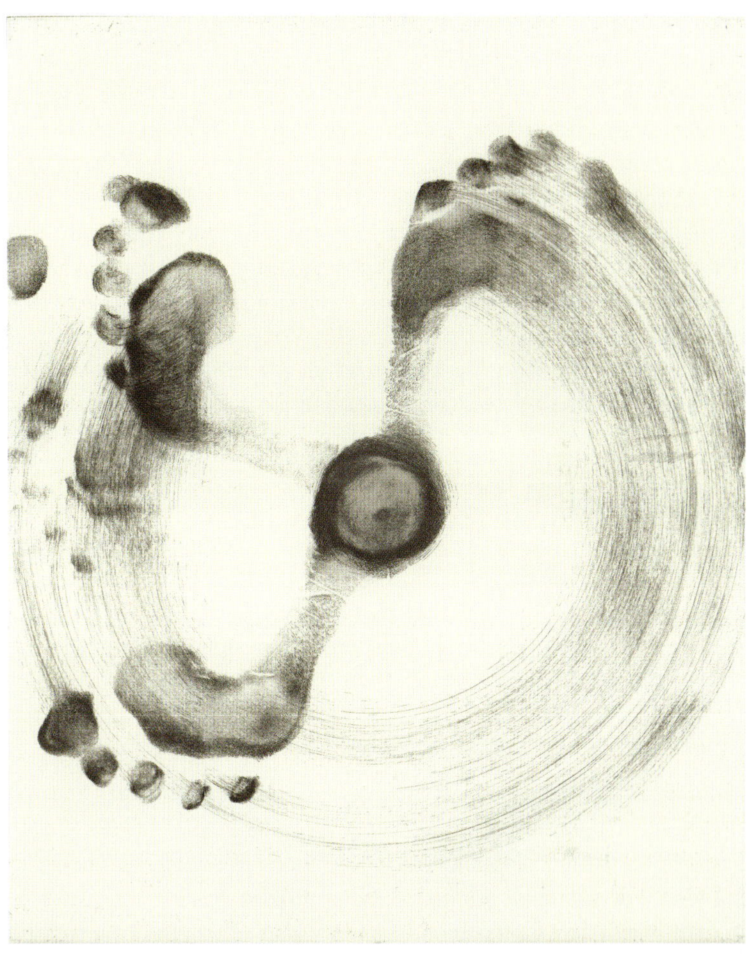

ILLUSTRATION 3.9 Trisha Brown, *Compass*, softground etching with relief roll, 2006. Courtesy of Graphicstudio, University of South Florida, Tampa, Florida.

Brown (1936–2017) correlated methods of notating dance movements – that is, choreography – with the idea that these visual notes could also be body traces (Illustration 3.9).

Applying choreographic notation to the bodily indices and the bodily traces that make up drawings reveals the significance of rhythm, pressure, sequence and, most important, breaks, pauses and absences for the idea of drawing as trace. There are many historical

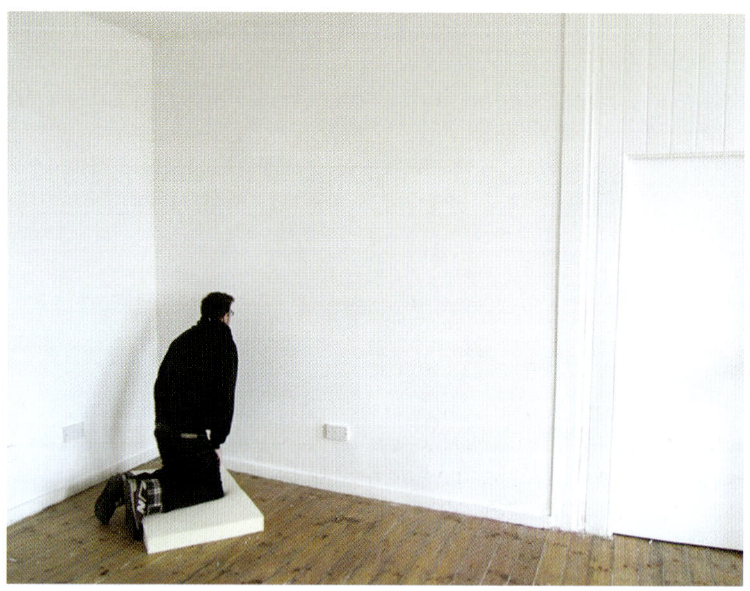

ILLUSTRATION 3.10 Robert Luzar, *Placing A Pause By Kneeling & Staring At Two Holes In The Wall/Try & Make One Whole From Two*, performance installation, 2011. From the exhibition *Sisyphus Happy*, Backlit Gallery, courtesy of the artist.

systems of choreographic notation by which a drawn trace can be described. These notation systems have their own symbols and systems of relationships for recording body movements, including stillness. For example, the single marked point, 'period' or 'full stop' is frequently used, sometimes isolated within brackets, to indicate a pause in movement. These symbols and systems have sometimes been incorporated into drawings themselves, in order to isolate and make visible very specific body movements or actions, as in the work of artist Robert Luzar (b.1980) (Illustration 3.10).

The differences between speech and writing can also be illuminating here. Drawn marks are different from speech or song because they remain as traces of bodily activity. Drawn marks frequently outlast the gestures that produced them. Vocal sounds, on the other hand, quickly dissipate to silence. However, speech and writing both make different types of body traces. The gestures that make up writing are traced by marks, which survive the gesture. The gestures that make up speech are only traced in air and do not survive.

Historically, discussions about the significance of this difference have overlooked the scribing aspect of writing, in large part because of the advent of print technology, which interposed between the marking body and the reader, removing body trace. Printing is indexical, providing ways of pointing to the past presence of the writer's body whilst not employing its literal traces.

Handwriting traces the sequence, rhythm and character of the past gestures that the writer used to draw the marks. The cadence of speech and the cadence of handwriting are equivalent. That is, the unique sequence, rhythm and character of each is visible in writing or audible in speech. On the other hand, printed words are also traces of the people, activities and situations in which they were produced, but they technically mediate between the bodily activities that accumulate to create and work machines to such a degree that they cannot be thought of as individual body traces. They might be thought of as the traces of group activity, as we have seen. Printed writing is not the equivalent of recorded speech. Rather, printed writing is the equivalent of machine-generated speech.

Trace and depiction

The current focus on thinking about drawing, as a trace of the body, might seem to diminish the status of depiction in drawing activities because the significance of the mark is seen to lie in recording the body rather than in visualizing an object. In practice, drawing today is made richer by the accumulation of these different ideas. Because there are many purposes for which drawings are made, the possibility of recording traces of the body, whilst also depicting the body, today offers fertile ground for development by all drafters in all drawing media. Drawing currently revises and reinvigorates its older traditions and ideas. An interest in gesture now combines the idea of direct trace with the possibility of depicting the body.

For example, the work of artist Jenny Saville (b.1950) explicitly connects the visible properties of the marks that she makes and the

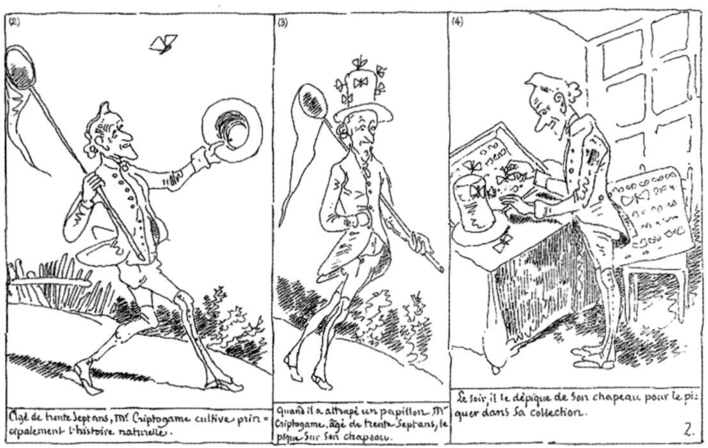

ILLUSTRATION 3.11 Rudolphe Töpffer, *Monsieur Criptogame*, ink on paper, 1845.

physical characteristics of the people and things that she depicts. This revises an older concept that visible gesture is non-verbal and meaningful independent of speech, found in the eighteenth century in the work of dramatist, novelist and philosopher Gotthold Lessing (1729–1781). In part, Lessing proposed that there is a grammar and vocabulary of postures and gestures that everyone shares – a common language of gestures. He used this idea as the foundation for a theory of dramatic performance. Lessing's work underpinned the emergence of a new drawing medium, the comic strip, in the drawings of Rudolphe Töpffer (1799–1846) in the early nineteenth century (Illustration 3.11).

Characteristics of the drafter's bodily movement create the character of the drawn mark and also create the character or the scene that the viewer imagines that they see in a depiction. Ways of showing unfolding action in drawings, exemplified in changing gestures, only emerged with the beginning of the comic strip. Töpffer based the drawn gestures of his comic strip characters on illustrations to Henry Siddons's (1774–1815) manual of acting. This manual showed an established set of images of gestures and body postures representing specific emotions in stage melodrama.

The modern connection between drawings that both trace the body and also depict bodies has its origin in Lessing and Töpffer, and has developed into a sophisticated tradition of contemporary fine art that combines performance, mark making and visualization. That the drafter's moving body leaves a trace – which can now also be understood to double as a depiction of a moving body, or bodies – is evidenced in the work of many contemporary artists, such as Jennie Saville (b.1970) and William Kentridge (b.1955), or in the work of Kara Walker (b.1969), where the marking traces of the artist's body are cuts depicting silhouettes.

4
STORY

If the trace of the drafter's body has gradually come to be thought of as meaningful, then it has only been a small step to propose that drawings exist in time as well as space because the body is never still. There are at least four different aspects to this.

First, the scenes that depictive drawings show must have a past and a future, although these are not shown in the depiction. Famously, philosopher Nelson Goodman (1906–1998) explained that when we look at a drawing of a tree, we also know that the tree was a seed and that it will eventually die and disappear, although none of these events are shown in the drawing.

Second, the marks that make a drawing always trace the duration of their making, as part of the tracing of the bodies that make them. Although a drawn mark has no duration, it traces duration.

Third, the time taken by the drafter to make a drawing is quite distinct from the time in the scene that the drawing depicts. This is easy to imagine, because we see a scene in its own time rather than the time in which the drawing was made. However, this is also the case with any set of drawn marks, even if they do not depict anything, because drawings also incorporate another distinct time, which is the time in which they are viewed.

Realizations of the four ways in which drawings represent time, prompted by the significance of the drafter's body, have introduced ideas of the ways in which drawings show stories.

Although there is a wide range of words describing what a story is, these often share the idea that 'story' encompasses everything that is told or shown by the creators of the story, distinct from the activities that they undertake to tell or show a story. This is not as simple as the commonly held distinction between form and content might have us believe. Rather, a story is always a bundle of different times. The time of the story and the time it takes for the story to be shown or told are only two of the significant relative times that must be in the bundle for a story to be a story.

Thinking about drawings as stories is very recent indeed. It crosses long-established boundaries between ideas about language, speech and writing, and ideas about the visual and performing arts. Plato's division of visual and verbal images into categories of visual space (or showing) and verbal time (or telling) is still entrenched in some academic disciplines, such as the study of art history or the study of English literature, although the division is continually contradicted in studies of media, narrative and games. These disciplines have found other ways of explaining the capacities of words and images and the relationships between them.

By thinking of drawings as bundles of different types of times (in which activities and things make their appearance), drafters and thinkers have recognized that drawings show stories that unfold in time. They have acknowledged that drawings can represent the unfolding of events in different times, in which the making of the drawing, what the drawing shows, the past and future of what is shown (if it is a depiction) and the time in which the drawing is viewed are all meaningful.

This way of thinking about drawing has been developed by historians of media such as Jan Baetens (b.1957) and Philippe Marion (b.1960), building upon earlier ideas about storytelling in the work of Harald Weinrich (b.1927), Seymour Chatman (1928–2015) and André Gaudreault (b.1952) and, subsequently, developing drawing-specific ideas of the ways in which these different times relate to each other and interact with each other.

One of the most influential of these ideas recasts the drafter as a visual narrator in a system of relationships between the different activities involved in showing a visual story, and the drawing as an 'utterance', or a unit of communication, which is produced and consumed in this relationship. Drawings have been described as stories when they establish the significance of the drafter as a narrator, above and beyond the significance of the drafter's body and, following this, the significance of thinking of the drawing as showing a story.

Written stories and drawn stories are similar in some respects. Stories in both media involve action and description. Written verbs and visibly depicted actions perform similar functions. They represent changes in characters and things. Descriptive writing provides information about everything besides the action in a story. In depictive drawings, this information is provided by everything that is shown – that can be seen – in the depiction.

However, writing and depiction also differ. A written story about a horse race might relate the actions of the crowd and horses whilst also describing the racecourse, the time of day of the race and the colours worn by the jockeys. The action can be related without descriptive writing. In a depictive drawing of the same horse race, the action is visualized as occurring at a particular time and place. The action cannot be shown without visual description. Every running horse that is drawn is a particular running horse. Everything about it is plain for the viewer to see (Illustration 4.1).

Descriptive drawing underpins the viewer's sense of the specific detail of an unfolding drawn story. Descriptive aspects of drawings can appear alongside, within or around depicted actions in a drawn story, in any degree of mixture – more or less descriptive or active – in the same drawing. In a drawing of a horse race, descriptive drawing shows the viewer everything that there is to be seen, including invisible information that can be inferred from what is seen – if the depicted day is sunny or cloudy or if the race is taking place in 1850 or 1920, for example.

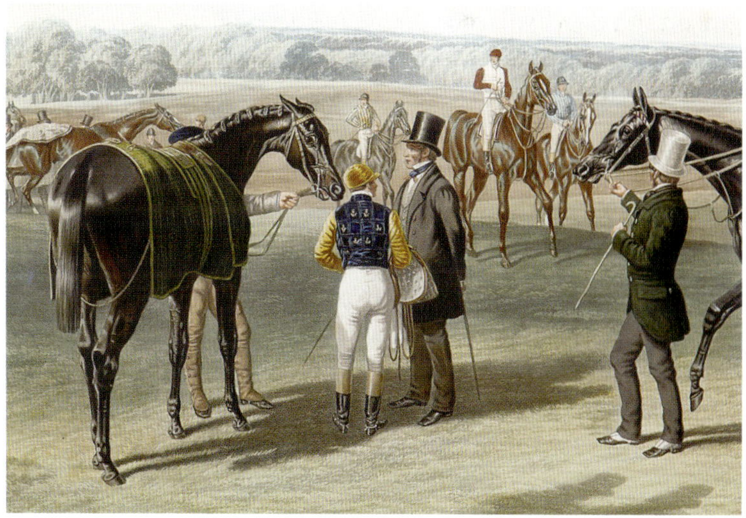

ILLUSTRATION 4.1 Anonymous, *Horse Racing*, colour lithograph, 1850.

Visual description can play a key role in determining the emotional tone of a drawn story or can provide information about a specific historic time or a specific place. These provide vital clues to the possibilities and impossibilities of the visual world in which the actions of the story take place. A drawing that shows events (as visible actions) on a snowy mountain in winter (as a visible description) holds very different possibilities than a drawing that shows the same events taking place in a Victorian drawing room.

In a drawn story, this relationship between visible description and visible action produces an effect on a viewer that is akin to a performance, in that a precise but changeable sense of witnessing and visually engaging with the passage of time characterizes both.

One school of thought currently describes how this effect becomes specific in drawn stories, as distinct from other visual media, such as movie media, for example. Philippe Marion brings together ideas of the drawn trace of the drafter's body, from art theory, plus ideas about the structure of visual storytelling. He proposes that all of the different relationships, representing time in drawn stories, are focused by the viewer's experience of the drawn trace. This includes any and all marks that the drafter makes, including writing. As a result, Marion thinks that the characteristics of the marks reproduce a range of emotional, material and bodily relationships, including the unfolding progress of depicted action and visual description, the style of the drawing and the relationship between the viewer and the drawing.

Story and point of view

Marion's approach to thinking about drawing greatly increases the importance of point of view. It fixes the location of the viewer. This is easier to understand in the case of drawings that show scenes because the viewer of the drawing is placed relative to the visible parts of the scene. When we look at a drawing of an aerial scene, we regularly talk about seeing the view 'from above'. In fact, viewers of drawings, wherever they actually are, are only located 'above' relative to what is shown. What is really surprising is that we aren't above at all. It is the drawing alone that articulates our view.

In Edgar Degas's (1834–1917) drawings of circus high-wire performers, the artist shows us a story in which we feel grounded because we see that the action takes place high above. Manipulation of point of view is one of the most powerful tools at the drafter's disposal.

Drawings of memories and of emotional and psychological conditions also fit this description of the significance of point of view. Point of view determines the location of the viewer, relative to what the viewer can see of the story. Therefore, it also determines the types of relationship that a viewer can have with characters in the story. The drafter sometimes manages a viewer's point of view so that it is the same as a character's point of view. Combinations of characters' and viewer's different points of view are also commonplace in drawn stories, creating the widest range of emotional and psychological effects. These effects have parallels in written literature that presents the thoughts of a character in a story.

Point of view produces all of the relationships between the viewer and the story. It also produces effects upon the viewer that suggest the subjective opinions of the drafter because the ways and means of making a drawing change each other. Therefore, the decisions that the drafter makes, about where and how to place marks on a surface, are guided by the importance of point of view. In making larger and smaller marks, the drafter connects point of view, types of mark and types of action seamlessly together. This variety often demonstrates different characteristics of marks made by drawing tools in different ways, when they are manipulated by either the drafter's fingers, wrist, elbow or shoulder. To return to the comment by illustrator Quentin Blake, quoted in the Introduction: 'The other bit of your mind is thinking, "Is this in the right place on the page?"'

The story of the drawing

I have touched upon the connections that have been made between the line (as a type of mark), movement and the progress of a story. One idea of the marked surface considers marks to be imagined as they are traced. As each mark is drawn, the drawing is discovered and each mark is a trace of this discovery. Rather than linking a series of known goals, each drawn mark transforms the drawing by changing what has gone before, such as the unmarked surface changed by the addition of one mark, then two marks, then three, etc. Hence, each mark establishes a past and a future for the drawing, in the traces of what has gone before and in anticipation of future marks. This structure, not only comprising sequences but also causes and consequences, is also characteristic of stories.

On this basis, the accumulation of drawn marks shows the story of the drawing's origin in the accumulated bodily capacities of the drafter, as much as each mark is a trace of the duration of the gesture that makes the mark. The accumulation of marks traces a sequence of gestures and the relationship between past gestures, continuing gestures and future gestures. For viewers of a drawing, including the drafter as the first viewer, the accumulated traces of accumulated gestures provide part of the significance of the drawing. The viewer can follow along the traced paths of these gestures, to reconstruct the sequences and types of gesture of the drafter and hence the past-to-present emergence of the drawing as an accumulation of marks.

The relationship between the layout of accumulated marks and the composition of a drawn scene once more mirrors the ways in which drawn depictions appear. The viewer both sees the marks on the page and imagines that they are seeing the depicted scene. The layout of the marks has a direct correlation with the layout of the imagined scene. The viewer imagines that they can see some things and not others, that they can see relative distances, nearer or further away, relative locations and height. All of these visualizations are directly related to the way in which the drawing has been made and to its purpose, represented in its layout on the surface. This specific relationship between graphic layout and scene setting is experienced most frequently in the medium of comics, although any meaningful array of drawn marks always involves this relationship.

Story and style

The way in which a drawing is made also has a profound impact on what the drawing shows. This idea is one of the innovations that thinking about drawings as stories has recently brought to maturity. It is only recently that drafters have started to apply current thinking about stories to drawings, borrowing from studies of literature, movie and language. Sometimes, we are so used to seeing a type of story shown in a specific way that we are confused, disoriented or even shocked when we see it shown in another way.

For example, the character Tintin, created by Hergé (George Remi [1907–1983]), is impossible to imagine without also imagining the way in which he is drawn, in a style of drawing that has come to be known as 'clear line'. The style and the whole world of the character are intimately bound to each other. However, as a character, Tintin can be drawn in many other ways whilst still remaining ostensibly Tintin. The association of one style with the character and his world is so strong that drawings made of Tintin in other ways, by other drafters, have had the power to outrage as well as upset readers (Illustration 4.2).

This also works the other way around. When we see specific ways of drawing, we expect to see the types of story with which these ways of drawing are associated. We all make these assumptions and they always have an ethical dimension. When we assume that a type of story and a type of drawing go together, we always overlook the fact that other people draw other stories in other ways.

For example, relatively early in the life of the architectural drawing system AutoCAD, which was launched in 1982, the system provided drafters with consistent items, called 'blocks' (Illustration 4.3). These 'blocks' were designed to provide a modular tool kit of recognizable items that could be used again and again, such as a range of trees, public furniture (such as park benches) and people depicted undertaking public activities (such as walking, jogging and sitting). After forty years of global use, these drawings have fixed the appearance of public life in the popular imagination, as visioned by architects and urban planners.

In 2015, architects Francisco Garcia Triviño, José Manuel López Ujaque and others developed series of alternative 'blocks', depicting a wide range of people who are never seen in AutoCAD. These included homeless people, overweight people, people engaged in a range of activities that are unseen in the 'blocks' and people with a range of racial, sexual and gender identities and even, possibly, political views. The drawing style of 'blocks' is maintained, however, so that the proposed shifts in the possible visions of buildings and designed spaces, provided by the AutoCAD style of drawing, immediately took on the appearance of authority, of reality.

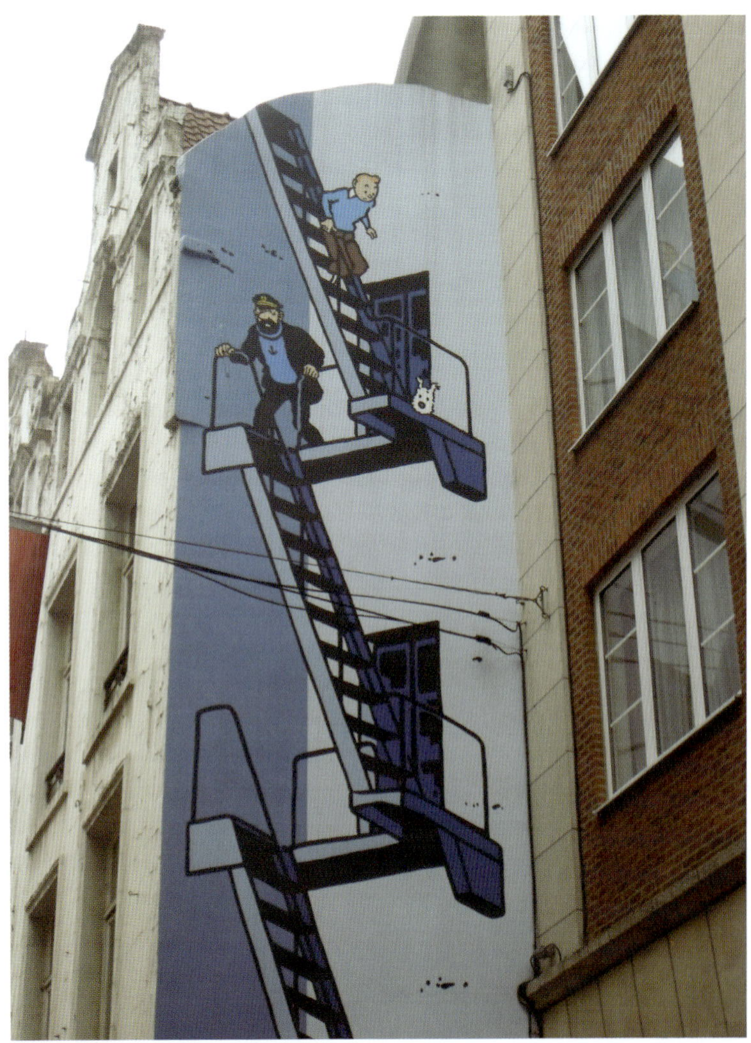

ILLUSTRATION 4.2 Hergé, *The Adventures of Tintin*, painted mural at Rue de l'Etuve, Brussels, 2011. Photograph by Ferran Cornella.

The way in which a viewer imagines the scene is influenced by the way in which the scene is drawn, or the drawing's style. Style is the specific degrees to which the manufacture of an individual drawing resembles or differs from the manufacture of other drawings. Consider any drawing where the depicted scene conforms to familiar ideas of what is shown,

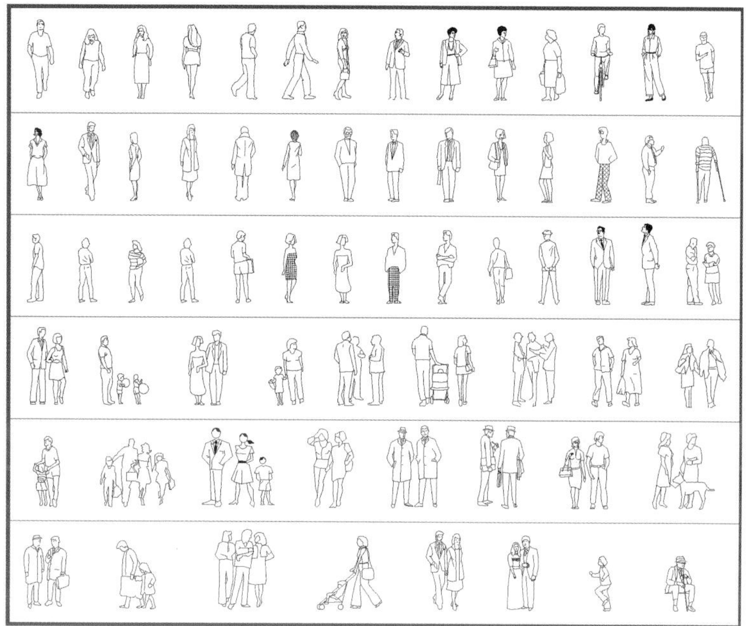

ILLUSTRATION 4.3 AutoCAD, *People CAD Blocks – Elevation View*, digital, 2020.

such as a Renaissance drawing of Adam and Eve. The consistency of the items shown in these scenes is striking, often in thousands of different drawings made over hundreds of years by many different drafters, for many different reasons. However, the styles in which these scenes are produced vary widely. In comparing a drawing of Adam and Eve from tenth-century Ethiopia, with a drawing of Adam and Eve from a collection of twenty-first-century clip art, almost every aspect of the manufacture of the drawing is different, but the represented scene is very similar (Illustrations 4.4 and 4.5).

As a result, the emotional character and specific significance of the scene varies widely, as it has always done for viewers of drawings made in different times and places, by different means and for different purposes. The scene can be considered to be the same because the items that make it up are recognizable. They can be ticked off from the same list. This is the case despite the differences in manufacture of the different drawings in which they appear. However, the opinions,

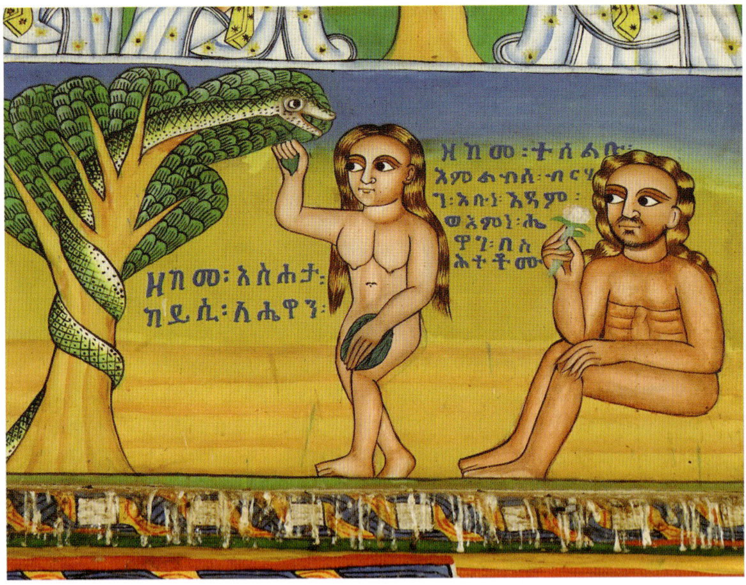

ILLUSTRATION 4.4 Anonymous, *Adam & Eve & the Serpent*, Facade of |
Yesus Church, Aksum, Ethiopia, 2013. Photograph by Adam Jones. Licensed
under CCBY-SA 2.0.

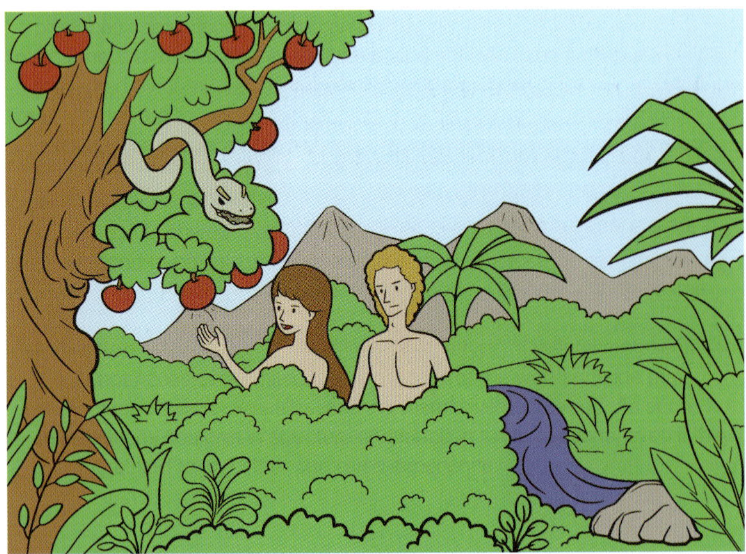

ILLUSTRATION 4.5 Openclipart, *Adam and Eve*, digital, 2020. Licensed under
CC O 1.0.

ideas and feelings prompted and represented by these differences in style are paramount. Each style shows a different set of these opinions, ideas and feelings.

Drawing style and character

The way in which the drafter draws a mark is just one story-drawing activity that can be thought of in terms of style. A simple example is found in the ways in which particular drawing traditions involve the collaboration of a number of drafters rather than a single drafter. In drawings that involve team production, such as animation, the style of the drawing can be viewed as collaborative as much as individual. Collaborative style is a set of manufacturing conventions that all of the drafters agree upon. Collaboratively, both the residual trace (if this remains) and the indexing of the network of drafter's bodies sit within this agreed framework. Ways of drawing are agreed upon and adopted, with trace and index more or less significant within the constraints that have been established.

Hence, the relationship between style and story, or the impact of style upon the story, is really the relationship between the specific ways in which a drawing is made and the story it shows. With collaborative drawings, the significance of individual drawing style can only be judged as part of the whole character of a production, including the ways in which the agreed stylistic constraints have an impact upon the story.

Differences in drawing style, in the same drawing or set of drawings, for example, are often used to highlight significant changes in a drawn story. They prompt questions about the status of the drafter and the status of the story. Drawing styles are associated with particular artists, historical periods and types of stories. Changing a drawing style changes these associations. Remaking an existing drawing in another style can produce surprising changes in the way in which characters and situations are understood in visual stories (Illustration 4.6). Often, stylistic changes indicate changes in points of view or characterization, not simply in the progress of the story but also in the way in which attitudes or emotions change. This idea has recently been explored by literature scholar Kai Mikkonen (b.1966).

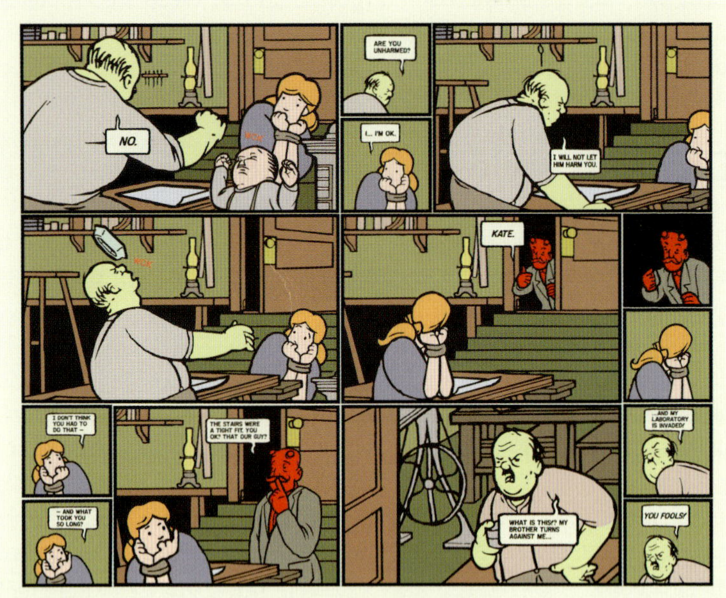

ILLUSTRATION 4.6 Simon Grennan, *Demonstration One (b) Mignola as Ware*, digital, 2009.

In this way, changes in drawing style can also create associations between a particular style and the thoughts, emotions or state of mind of a character. Changes in drawing style are understood to indicate changes in the consciousness of a character in the story. In David Mazzucchelli's (b.1960) graphic novel *Asterios Polyp*, published in 2009, different characters in the story are consistently drawn in their own style; however, they interact with other characters, drawn in different styles. These different styles become metaphors for different characteristics, consistently belonging to different characters. Further, this association of drawing style with the mind of a character suggests to viewers that the characters themselves have influence over the ways in which the story develops, as well as the way in which the story is shown.

This is essentially a comparative effect, in which the viewer identifies different styles and changes in style by comparing them with others. The style in which a story is drawn also always refers to other styles in which stories have been drawn in the past. As a result, combinations of memories and emotions govern the viewing of all drawn stories, partly derived from the character of the depicted scene and partly derived from the style of the drawing.

For example, in the 2016 graphic novel *The Call of Cthulhu (For Beginning Readers)*, R. J. Ivankovic presents a visual adaptation of H. P. Lovecraft's famous horror story *The Call of Cthulhu*, published in 1928. The drawings are made in the style of children's author, Dr Suess (Theodor Geisel, 1904–1991). Any expectations that the drawings are an adaptation of a well-known adult horror story are complicated by the fact that they appear to be drawings for children, made by Dr Suess. The contradictions between the content of the story and the style in which it is drawn are so great that they result in humour. In this instance, it is the incongruity of the different memories and emotions prompted by the scene and the style that are effective.

5
DRAWING TODAY

Today, drawing is characterized by changefulness. The wide range of ideas in the history of drawing, about its possibilities, its uses and the experiences that it provides, continues to maintain its flexibility and relevance. Drawing cannot be reduced to any one medium. Hence, technological changes deepen as well as widen its possibilities. Drawing activities also encompass large changes in ideas, continuing to make links with the past as much as they transform the present.

In the twenty-first century, drawing has guided the impact of digital technology rather than the other way around. Digital interfaces often employ ideas from drawing, placing touch, trace and index at the communication crossroads. The influence of drawing on digital technology has occurred despite the fact that the swipe of a touch screen or the airport body scan are underwritten by binary code – sequences of invisible electronic pulses, 'on' or 'off', represented by 'zero' and 'one'. We are far past the moment when the languages of computer programming seemed to be contradicted by flesh and blood. Digital technology is characterized by reproducible relationships, which are made between analogue activities and systematic patterns of code.

Ideas about drawing have migrated from the disciplines in which they developed and now pervade everything. One of the results of this has been an increasing hybridity of thinking about the possibilities of mark making, which brings together ideas from different disciplines. For example, the fast, light touch of the sketch can now deal with types of professional information once reserved for the textbook and drawn depictions. Far from being banished by systematic computer code, the sketch in fact underwrites the conception of virtual realities. In particular, from drawing, virtual reality seems to have learned to think about the ways in which it makes use of bodily resources. Likewise, visual storytelling has developed new processes by combining some very old ideas about the drafter's marks with some very new ways of thinking about collaboration and authorship, in movie animation, for example.

In the twenty-first century, a strong focus on describing drawing as a process has been challenged by a renewed interest in the symbolic and depictive capacities of drawing. Artists such as Callum Eaton (b.1997) and Toba Khedoori (b.1964) employ types of visual imitation that revive older debates about mimesis and illusion (Illustration 5.1).

At the same time, the long history of drawing itself still prompts the recurring idea that drawing taps into an authentic or fundamental shared humanity. This idea proposes that drawing can reach and represent human experiences that are beyond technology or differences in culture and which are consequently innocent because they are literally prehistoric. This idea is always rooted in specific circumstances, despite its claim to universality. Today, there remains a strong tradition of thinking about drawing as emblematic of a return to innocence, with twentieth-century roots in the European avant-garde, that is, artists, designers and drafters who used the idea to overturn earlier cultural conventions.

Artists such as Tracey Emin (b.1963) and Rosemary Trockel (b.1952) build upon the work of Louise Bourgeois (1911–2010) in trying to make drawings that make visible the complex emotional relationships between the drafter and society by adopting, rejecting and then transforming the traditional crafts of drawing (Illustration 5.2). Bourgeois herself provided a live link to a history of pre-Second World War psychological drawing. The twentieth-century tradition of drawing as a means of self-revelation, whilst also influenced by displays of unselfconsciousness, still prompts interest in the craft history of drawing.

Increasingly, late twentieth-century ideas about drawing and the body, which are now foundational, are being explored across media, in the creation of interfaces, in performances and in immersive environments. Drawing activities tie together the multimedia productions of both commercial movie studios, in animation and animation/live action, such as Studio Ghibli (the producer of *When Marnie Was There* [2014]) and Pixar (the producer of *Toy Story* [1995] and *WALL–E* [2008]). Drawing now encompasses both 2D and 3D animation, crossing older

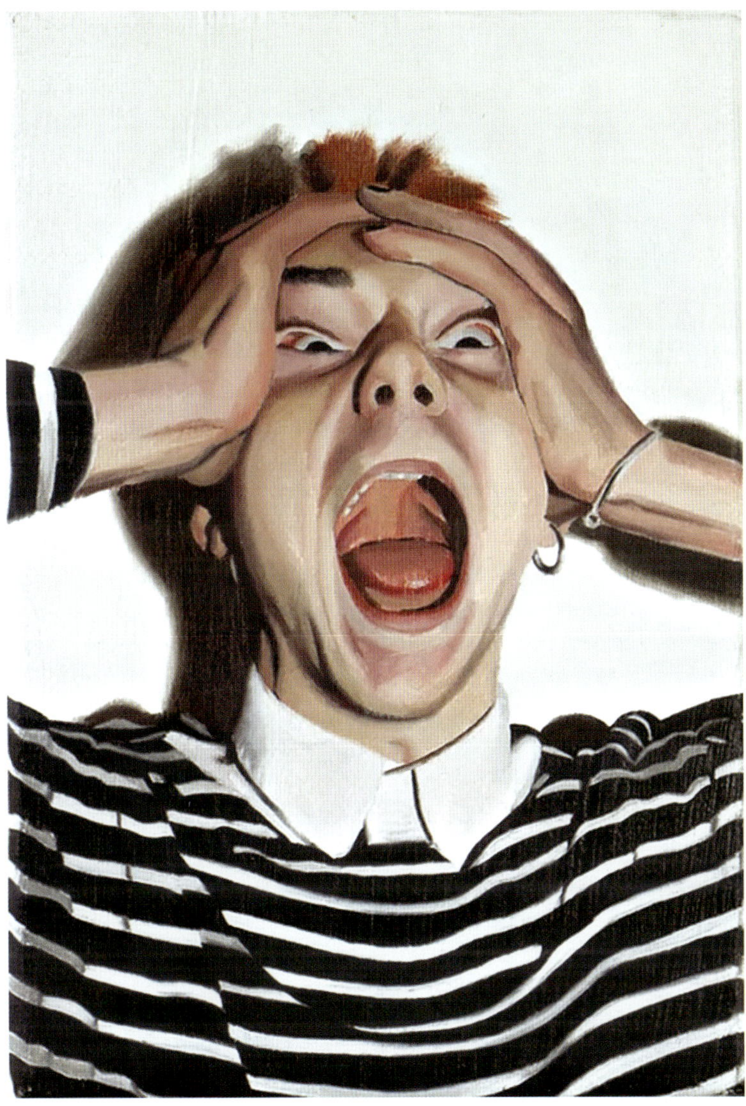

ILLUSTRATION 5.1 Callum Eaton, *The Scream*, oil on canvas, 2020. Courtesy of the artist.

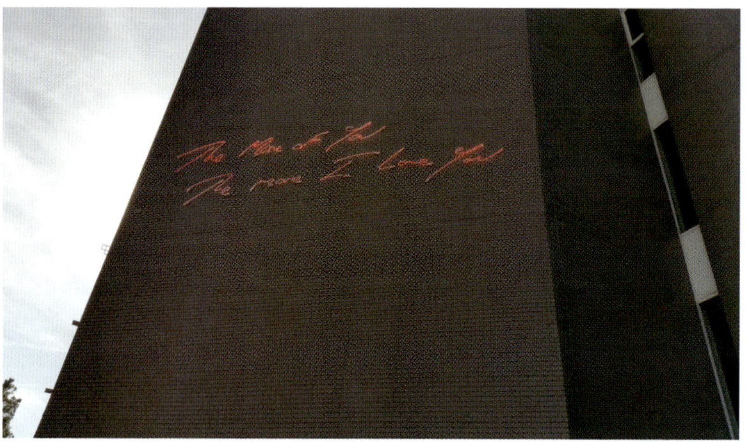

ILLUSTRATION 5.2 Tracey Emin, *The more of you the more I love you*, neon and glass, 2016. Photograph by Ceescamel. Licensed under CC BY-SA 2.0.

boundaries between ideas of the drafter's bodies, drawing systems, movement, trace and mark. In very similar ways, drawing also ties together the multimedia works of artists such as Kurt Adams (b.1980), who visibly extends the capacities of his body in time and space by 'supersizing' drawn marks as the basis for large-scale, immersive light projections, radically transforming his own body.

Today, media hybridity also means accumulation, over-writing and erasure, often with the aim of social or political change. The different media used by artist William Kentridge (b.1955) present visual equivalents to real-world power relationships, often placing drawings of the artist's body at the centre of multiple erasures and over-drawings. Sometimes resulting in animated films, Kentridge's hybrid drawings visualize the social and political conditions of South Africa. These techniques have deep roots in public drawing and public writing. Artist Dan Perjovschi (b.1961) makes use of millennia-old techniques of integrating unsanctioned drawings into the public realm as graffiti, frequently connecting the objects of the drawings to the locations in which he makes the drawings (at sites of conflict or places under strict control) and his own body. They are often physically inaccessible or placed large distances apart (Illustration 5.3).

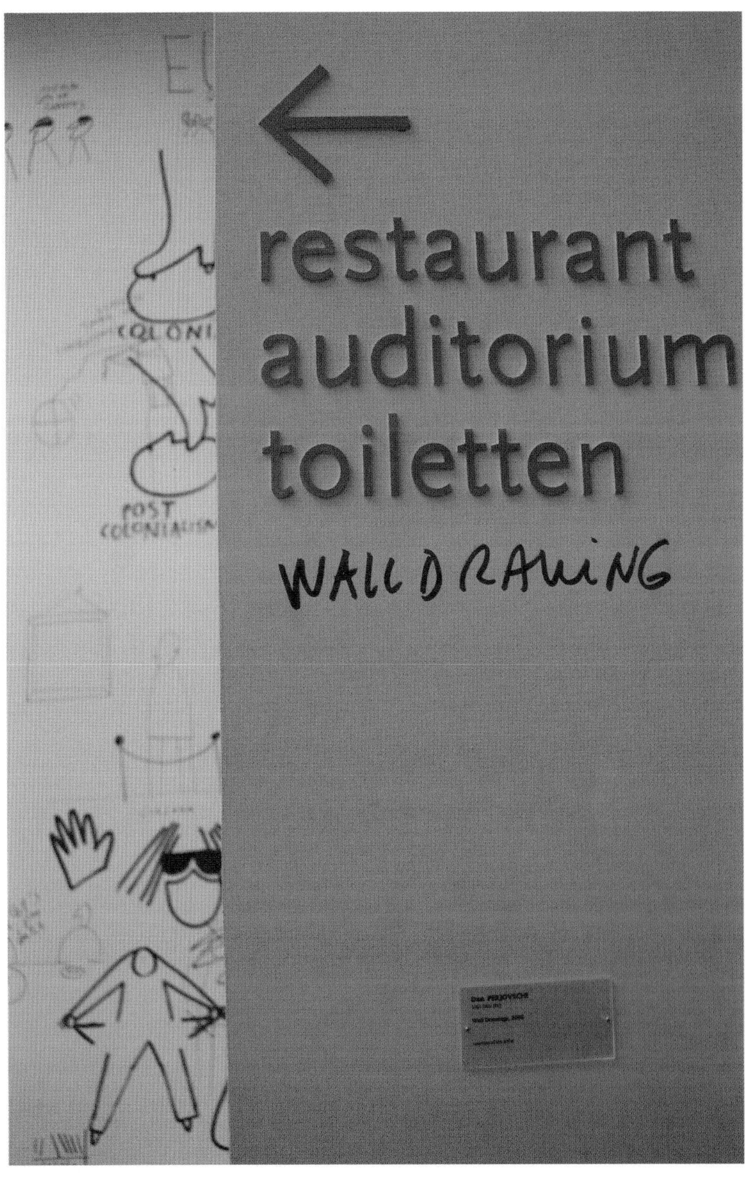

ILLUSTRATION 5.3 Dan Perjovschi, *Wall Drawing*, ink, 2010. Licensed under CC BY 2.0.

Feeling

Historically, drafters and others who think about drawing have not paid much attention to the feelings that making a drawing entails. Emphasis was placed upon the feelings of viewers, not drafters. The drafter was thought of as the 'first viewer' of a drawing. This assumed that the process of drawing was relatively insignificant when compared to the goal of achieving a complete drawing. The drafter was privileged to be able to see their drawing emerge, but the feelings that the process entailed were overlooked. Drafters were skilled, but what it felt like to be skilled – and whether this was of any importance – was either ignored or was described according to the feeling that their complete work prompted in viewers.

However, making and viewing are very different activities. Attention has turned to the physical, felt processes of drawing, as drafters start to place the body, social relationships and the environment at the centre of their drawing processes.

This shift in emphasis, from vision to feeling, has underwritten a revival in the idea that drafters feel pleasure in drawing, or that drawing might be more strongly associated with feelings of pleasure than other types of feeling. In part, this idea is founded upon two characteristics that many drawing activities share – immediacy and the capacity to hold a drafter's attention. Making a drawing is easy but complex. It is easy to make marks and, less simply, marks become drawings when the drafter recognizes that a mark represents, points to or records something else.

This combination of fundamental technical ease and maintaining the attention of the drafter is very beguiling. It is this combination that produces pleasure, sometimes known as a flow state, 'being in the zone' or, more accurately, feeling yourself feel. Whether pleasure is a sensation, a type of experience or a state of mind is still debated.

Feeling is often thought of as spontaneous emotion and sensation. However, feeling also encompasses some types of judgement that are not simply accompanied by spontaneously occurring emotions or sensations. These include ethical judgements of right and wrong, about which is commonly said 'I don't feel right about' a situation or 'it feels wrong'.

This definition of feeling also encompasses a definition of **aesthetics**. The word is borrowed from 'aesthesis', the Greek for 'sensation'. Aesthetic literally means 'sensational', which has a slightly different, though related, meaning in English ('exciting'). For some reason, English speakers understand the word 'anaesthetic' and are used to using it but are less sure of the word aesthetic. Anaesthetic means 'insensible', without sensation, 'unfeeling' and 'without feeling'. It is useful for identifying the meaning of its opposite – aesthetic.

> **AESTHETIC** Aesthetic is borrowed from 'aesthesis', the Greek for 'sensation'. Aesthetic literally means 'sensational', which has a slightly different, though related, English meaning ('exciting').

Even a brief summary of the historical debates about aesthetics, feeling and judgement would fill another book. It is enough to say that these debates have produced ideas on three topics: first, the relationship between judgement and spontaneously felt emotions and sensations; second, comparisons between emotion and sensation; and, third, ways of distinguishing emotions and sensations from others in an encompassing environment.

A further idea, which also runs through these debates, claims emotions spark responses to environmental changes (we cry or laugh through our body in reaction to something that has happened, for example) whilst at the same time emotions produce, modulate and transform the character of our environment, as much as our bodies are modulated and transformed in response. Every situation is an experience of emotion. Emotions are never absent, even if we don't pay attention to them.

These different changes of body and environment can be demonstrated using drawing as an example. A drafter experiences what it feels like to make a drawing. The drafter responds emotionally to the environmental changes brought about by making the drawing. However, the feelings of someone viewing the drawing come about quite differently. What it feels like to draw and what it feels like to see a drawing are not the same, although they might be related in significant ways.

The emotions of both drafters and viewers, in making and using a drawing, are not contained in the drawing. Rather, the drawing is more or less important as a prop (a theatre stage property) in an emotional situation of which it forms a part.

Thinking like this, the emotional possibilities of making and viewing drawings are significant according to the possible ways in which drawings are made and used. These possible ways of making and use are always attended by impossibilities. Sometimes these possibilities and impossibilities seem obvious. For example, before the invention of computers, it was impossible to make or view digital images and impossible to either feel emotional responses to them or to sense the emotional characteristics of a digital environment. The physical and social possibilities and impossibilities of a change in an environment, such as the advent of computers, also create emotional possibilities and impossibilities. Hence, we can consider drawing activities of all types as the historic appearance and transformation of emotional capacities.

Emotional experiences of different types of drawing activities (and different drawings) are an accumulation of specific possibilities of production, distributing and viewing (or, what is or is not possible), with any type of drawing. Even the most conventional, systematic or uniform ways of drawing both prompt and represent emotions. Because no situation is emotionally neutral, feelings also characterize drawing activities and drawings that are often described as unfeeling or emotionally cold.

There are clear distinctions between different types of drawing practices, according to differences in the possibilities and impossibilities different drawn forms offer and the different purposes to which they are put. These distinctions are also always emotional distinctions.

For example, consider three types of drawing where social and formal habits and expectations can also be described as emotional characteristics: fine art drawing, comic strips and engineering drawing. The descriptions of emotional characteristics that define these social and formal habits are not comprehensive, of course. Within the practices of making and viewing drawings, a range of emotions might characterize any situation. However, different practices are also supported by different and distinct social and formal habits and expectations, which are always emotional. That is, they have significant emotional characteristics that help to define them.

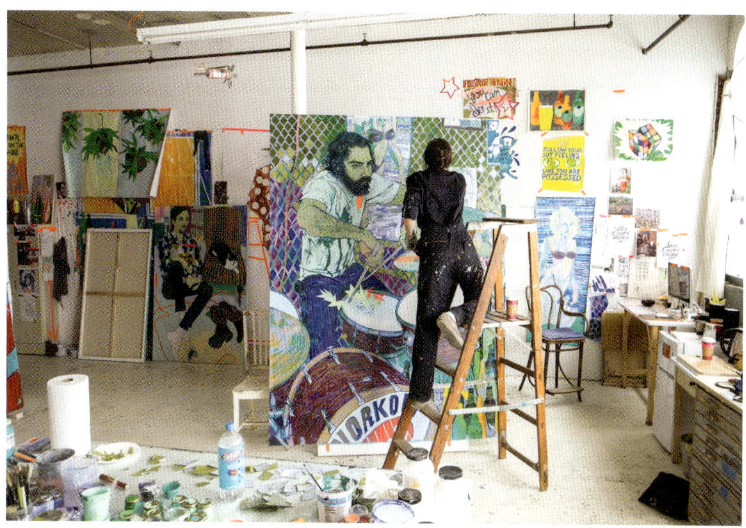

ILLUSTRATION 5.4 Don Stahl, *Hope Gangloff in her studio*, photograph, 2015. Licensed under CC SA 4.0.

Fine art drawing derives from a range of diverse aims and fine art drawings display the widest variety of forms. However, these diverse examples share two things that make them recognizable. First, the function of the fine artist's studio and the art gallery mirror each other. In the art gallery, viewers literally place themselves in the position of the absent drafter to see a drawing. The drawings made in a fine art studio are fine art drawings. When we are in an art gallery, we expect drawings that we see to be fine art drawings. The activity of viewing a drawing replaces the activity of making a drawing (Illustration 5.4).

Second, fine art drawings are often considered to be unique commodities for sale, extending the substitution of production by the artist in the studio to consumption by the viewer in the gallery. This type of consumption is the same as viewing items that are (or were) available in a shop. An emotional description of these social and formal facts is generated by the social contract underpinning the recognition of fine art objects on the part of drafters and viewers: fear (of social exclusion and economic failure), shame (for accepting a social contract that has fundamentally financial motives) and, its inverse, pride (at having achieved recognition or made a sale, as much as made a good drawing).

On the other hand, the drawings that constitute comics largely aim to show stories. This locates comics in the history of storytelling. Comics have a place in literary traditions because comics and literature both form part of the history of the production and consumption of print media. The world of visual stories involves constant redrawing of visual properties and modifications of these properties in sequence, again and again. A conventional comics panel shows distinct moments in time. The next panel often shows only a slight modification – and on and on. On the part of the drafter, an emotional description of these facts reveals feelings of entrenchment, deferral, dread and relief, as foundational emotional characteristics of the practices of drawing comics. This is somewhat ironic, given that the comics medium reveals joy, lightheartedness and even happiness as the expected emotional characteristics of reading comics (Illustration 5.5).

Finally, an engineering drawing, made to guide the manufacture of a part of a machine, uses established visual, verbal and mathematical systems to identify and arrange information, most often within the overall code provided by digital media. Engineering drawings are always

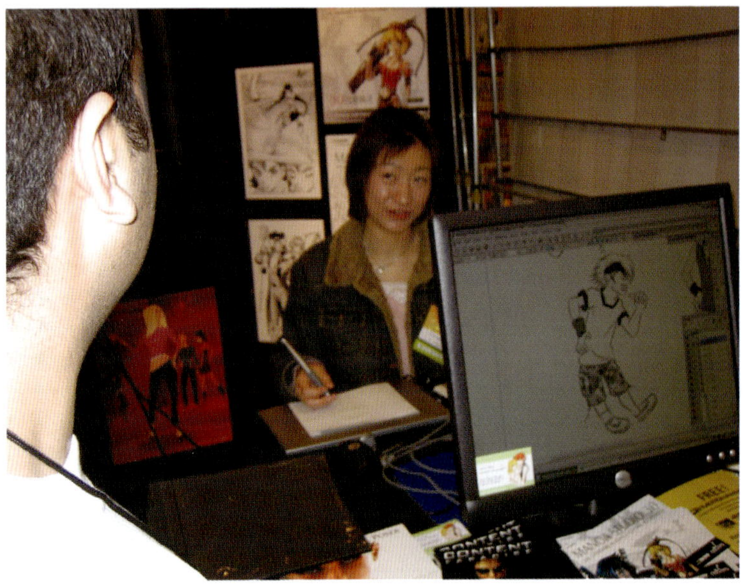

ILLUSTRATION 5.5 Mario Anima, *Manga Maker*, photograph, 2006. Licensed under CC BY 2.0.

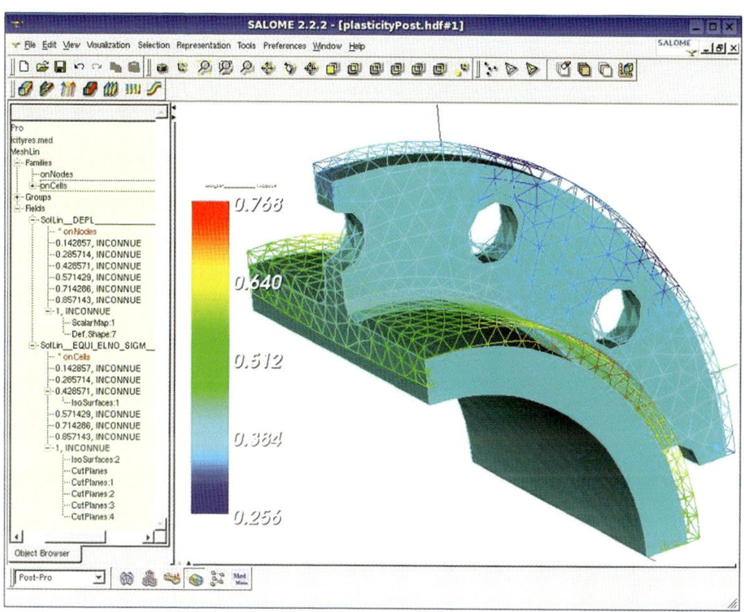

ILLUSTRATION 5.6 Joël Cugnoni, *Nonlinear statistics analysis of a 3D structure subjected to plastic deformations with Code-Aster*, screenshot, 2008. Licensed under GNU General Public License 2.0.

defined by part-to-part and part-to-whole relationships. They are components within an information system with a forward goal, to which they are essential but in which they are not included (Illustration 5.6). An emotional description of these facts reveals fear of failure to include and arrange information according to established rules. This emotion is only allayed by the less intense one of satisfaction in the drawing being adequate to its function.

The differences between these three sets of conditions characterize not only the situations in which different types of drawings are made and used but also the types of drawings we expect to encounter in these different situations. They also dictate their emotional characteristics. These emotions are also an expected part of the experience of these different types of drawings, on the part of drafters and viewers.

Of course, some aspects of these three different sets of circumstances are shared. Consequently, they might also share emotional characteristics. There are overlaps. However, drafters in the three different circumstances draw according to different aims and ideas, with different social, cultural and material resources available to them. The feelings that are produced in making drawings in these different times and places also differ from each other.

There is a wide variety of words used to describe the ways in which a drafter manipulates materials: touch, press, kiss, brush, pinch, stroke, bruise, push, tickle, slap, punch, hit, pummel or knead, for example. Each of these descriptions of different physical drawing activities is also a description of their different emotional characteristics, for the drafter – the clarity and straightforwardness of 'press' and 'knead', the intimacy of 'kiss', 'stroke', the playfulness of 'tickle', the aggression of 'slap' and 'pummel'.

Quantifying and distinguishing emotions is notoriously difficult. The more specific the description needs to be, the more difficult the task becomes. As a result, definitions of those emotions that have been easiest to recognize in a wide range of circumstances have remained constant (fear, anger, joy and sadness), whilst 'disgust' 'surprise' and 'contempt' are also sometimes singled out.

In fact, emotions are most frequently complex hybrids of a number of these because there is no generally applicable response to any situation. What makes one person feel angry will almost certainly make another person feel sad, surprised or angry/surprised.

A drafter's feelings about making a drawing derive from the possibilities and impossibilities for different thoughts and actions, presented by a specific set of circumstances, plus the unique ways in which the drafter's thoughts and the drafter's body interact with and transform these circumstances.

Emotions are physical responses to changes in the drafter's environment. These changes push the drafter off course, so to speak. Emotions are a physical way of attempting to regain that course. Recall the example of the comic strip drafter, repeating very similar drawings again and again, to meet deadline after deadline. Considering emotions as physical responses to changes in the drafter's equilibrium, the activity of drawing can be seen as a series of responses to a demanding, high-stress production environment. By making each drawing, the drafter goes some way to de-stressing. Each stroke of the pen decreases a sense of doom, incrementally restoring emotional balance. In this scenario, the drafter feels drawing as relief. Alternatively, the comic strip drafter might feel the opposite – that each stroke of the pen feels like another lash of the corporate whip, producing emotions attendant upon endurance, resignation or, at the end of the drafter's tether, desperation and anger. Either way, the emotional sensations the drafter feels, when making a drawing, are physical responses that adjust the drafter's course.

Drawing activities produce sensations, ideas and visual representations that are related to each other. It is possible for a drafter to make a joyful-seeming drawing when angry, or an angry-seeming drawing when joyful. However, the relative anger or joy represented in the drawing disturbs, or makes more complex, the represented emotion and the felt emotion. Part of the performance of drawing activities is self-performance, or the pleasure of feeling yourself feel. Drawing anger, the drafter does not become angry but does experience anger (Illustration 5.7).

ILLUSTRATION 5.7 Twitter Emoji Project, *Angry*, svg file, 2015. Licensed under CC BY 4.0.

By the same process, all drawings that attempt to represent emotions also carve out, identify and characterize the drafter as well as the drawing. The drafter's attempts to get back on course, through the production of emotions, changes their body when drawing emotional sensations. Drawings also trace the struggle to get back on course itself. As a result, when a viewer sees a drawing of emotion, they also have the sensation of feeling the drafter's feelings and of understanding that viewing their emerging drawing of an emotional topic finally has an effect on the drafter as well.

Technology old and new

New types of materials and new technology are extending and reforming relationships between media, body and environment. While commonplace ideas about drawing continue to repeat the historic emphasis upon the drafter's hand, or intuition, or the directly traced evidence of the drawn mark, new technology and new materials have played a pivotal role at every stage in the history of drawing. No less than digital technology, in the twentieth century, the development of printing technology, in the fifteenth century, produced new ideas of drawing media, new ideas of how drawings are used and new ideas of the capacities of the drafter's body.

Revised opinions about established historical ideas and methods of drawing now form the keystone of new approaches. Since the 1980s, a handful of artists have made use of old drawing technology to comment upon the experiences left behind, overlooked or rendered inaccessible by new drawing technology.

Recent revivals of older craft technology have produced a reaction and a school of self-consciously 'dumb' drawing has emerged. This approach to drawing avoids the appearance of craft skill, creating the idea that the drafter is untrained, as shown in the work of David Shrigley (b.1968). Paradoxically, this self-conscious artlessness demands a high degree of knowledge and technical experience to enable drafters to undertake a strategy of giving up their own skill.

On the other hand, the work of drafters such as Edward Allington (1951–2017) and, more recently, Pablo Bronstein (b.1977) exemplify a trend towards a reconsideration, reconfiguration and employment of older drawing technology and methods. Far from a nostalgic impulse, these drafters return to older methods in order to criticize and influence current dominant visions of society and culture. Bronstein has adopted a sophisticated and highly developed range of graphic techniques, borrowed from the seventeenth and eighteenth centuries. His drawings often make use of these techniques in incongruous ways, using them to depict the most up-to-date scenes. The pairing of old drawing craft and contemporary topics creates commentary on both the past and the present.

Systematic drawings

Contemporary drafters still employ drawing systems to analyse complex networks, plans and data through systematic visualization. The creation of contemporary drawing systems has left behind older aims of teaching, explaining and record-keeping, although a wide range of older systems remain in use.

On the one hand, contemporary systematic drawings are generated by the need to understand data, such as the drawings created by machines that measure the collisions of subatomic particles (Illustration 5.8). On the other hand, drafters often use systems to produce particular emotional effects on viewers rather than for the purpose of sorting or classifying information. Drafters Michael Ditchburn (b.1991) and Chris Ware (b.1967) use a very old spatial projection system called **axonometric**, in which parallel lines existing in the real world are always drawn as parallel lines on the surface. Both drafters sense the ways in which a viewer of their drawings feels constrained by this system and, as a result, are able to both reproduce and to comment upon the inescapable regularity and crushing uniformity of modern life.

AXONOMETRIC A drawing system in which parallel lines existing in the real world are always drawn as parallel, regardless of their perceived relative depth or their distance from the viewer. Axonometric systems often (but not always) rely upon the convention that, relative to each other, marks appearing lower in a drawing represent items that are nearer to the viewer than higher marks.

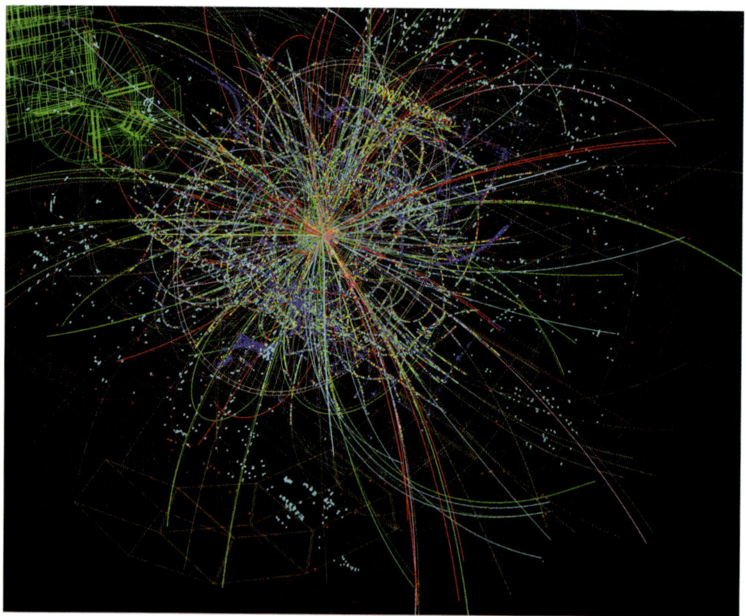

ILLUSTRATION 5.8 Anonymous, *First proton-lead ion collisions at the Large Hadron Collider*, digital drawing, 2014. Photograph by Charito Perez. Licensed under CC BY-SA 3.0.

Identity and power

The impact of waves of crises in identity (and the power relationships that these crises reveal) is increasing, in a social context that has been profoundly affected by awareness of social injustice and inequality. For example, Marcia Kure (b.1970) makes use of techniques and materials from both Western traditions of drawing and Nigerian traditions, creating juxtapositions that make visible historic and current colonial relationships and gender relationships (Illustration 5.9). Ellen Gallagher (b.1965) adopts the conventions of anthropological drawings to point to imbalances in the power relationships between scientists and their subjects. The association of particular craft traditions and particular drawing materials, with particular types of personal and cultural experience, is increasingly prevalent.

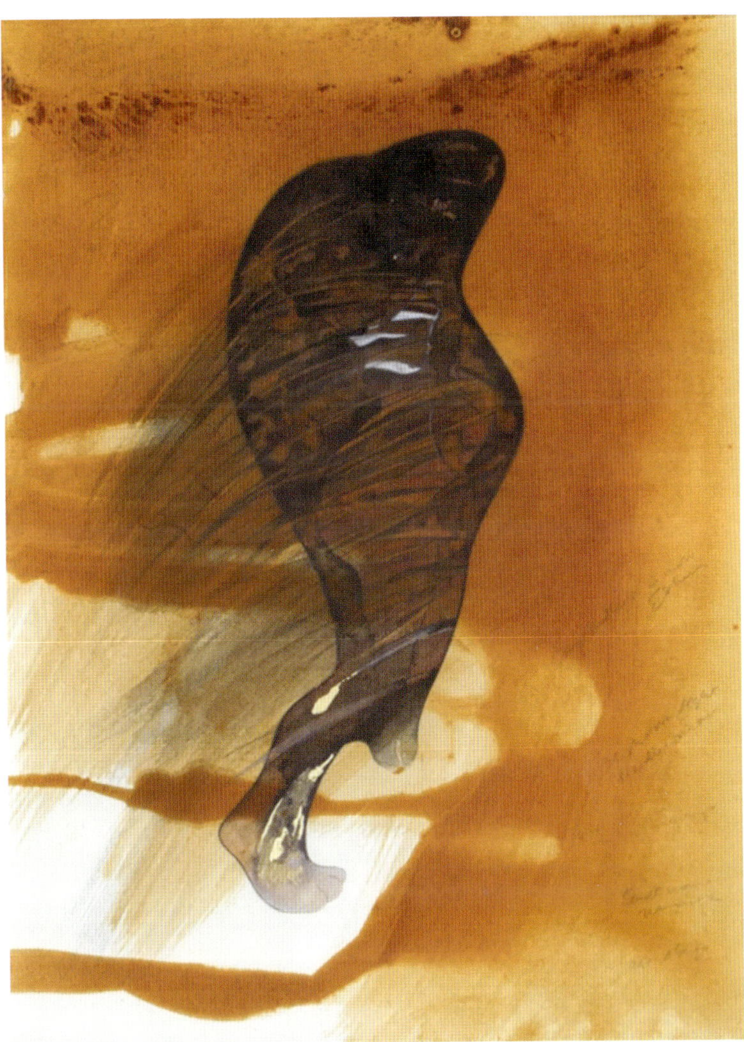

ILLUSTRATION 5.9 Marcia Kure, *Women of the Quilt I*, kolanut pigment, watercolour, gouache, ink, gold and pencil on paper, 2016. Courtesy of the artist and Rebecca Hicks.

Textiles and the line

The reclamation, by drafters, of types of drawing activities, materials and contexts long overlooked by male-dominated cultural and social history is proving fertile ground for the transformation of drawing. For example, weavers have long argued that textiles share with drawing some of the fundamental principles and the symbolic potential of line. Drawings by Nithikul Nimkulrat (b.1974) explicitly bring these principles together by using three-dimensional yarns as drawn lines (Illustration 5.10). Nimkulrat weaves, stitches and knots her works, frequently resulting in large-scale, three-dimensional drawings. These drawings

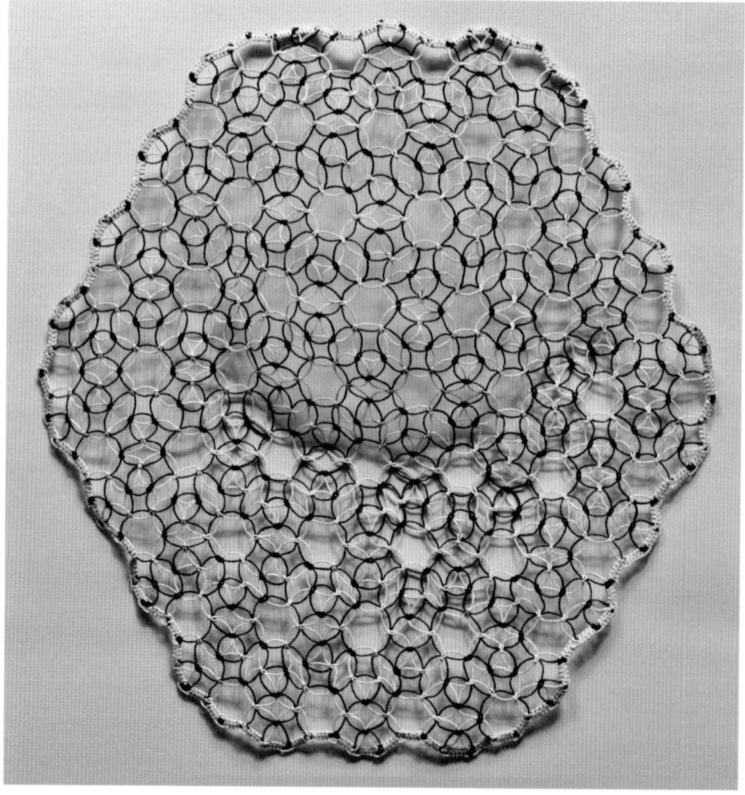

ILLUSTRATION 5.10 Nithikul Nimkulrat, *Rhombi Knots*, paper, string, 2018. Courtesy of the artist.

refer to the ways in which women weavers continue to visualize and produce their own and other's bodies through textiles.

Conjecture and hypothesis

Recently, the speculative aspects of drawing, which used to fall largely within the idea of drawings as preparation for future activities – that is, planning and modelling – are emerging as methods of analysis and types of knowledge in themselves. Types of drawings that might have been hidden or discarded as part of the process of making another object are increasingly included in the final work (such as the technical drawings made to direct the production of every type of object, from a bucket to a jet engine, or to direct the production of a painting). Architects plans, for instance those made by Zaha Hadid (1950–2016), are often now used to create a public sense of the buildings that they have helped to build. Artists such as Dan McCleary (b.1952) exhibit preparatory drawings as aspects of final, multipart works.

Collaborative drawing

Often inspired by ideas about the body in society, a new tradition of collaborative drawing has developed in the last thirty years, which aims to test and transform social relationships by using drawing methods and concepts as catalysts. Drawing is often used to describe, record or change encounters between different people, or to focus attention on the ways in which conventional encounters take place. Artist Jen Southern (b.1966) has used Global Positioning Systems (GPS) to draw together, literally, the activities of people remote from one another. Often, collaborative drawing derives its methods from people's history (previously called spoken history or oral history), making use of both personal stories and the experiences of storytellers as a source for drawings in which all or some participants will speak and/or draw. Kateřina Šedá (b.1977) facilitates other people drawing from memory, alongside her, in order to make use of the emerging drawn images as references to past emotions, times, people and places (Illustration 5.11).

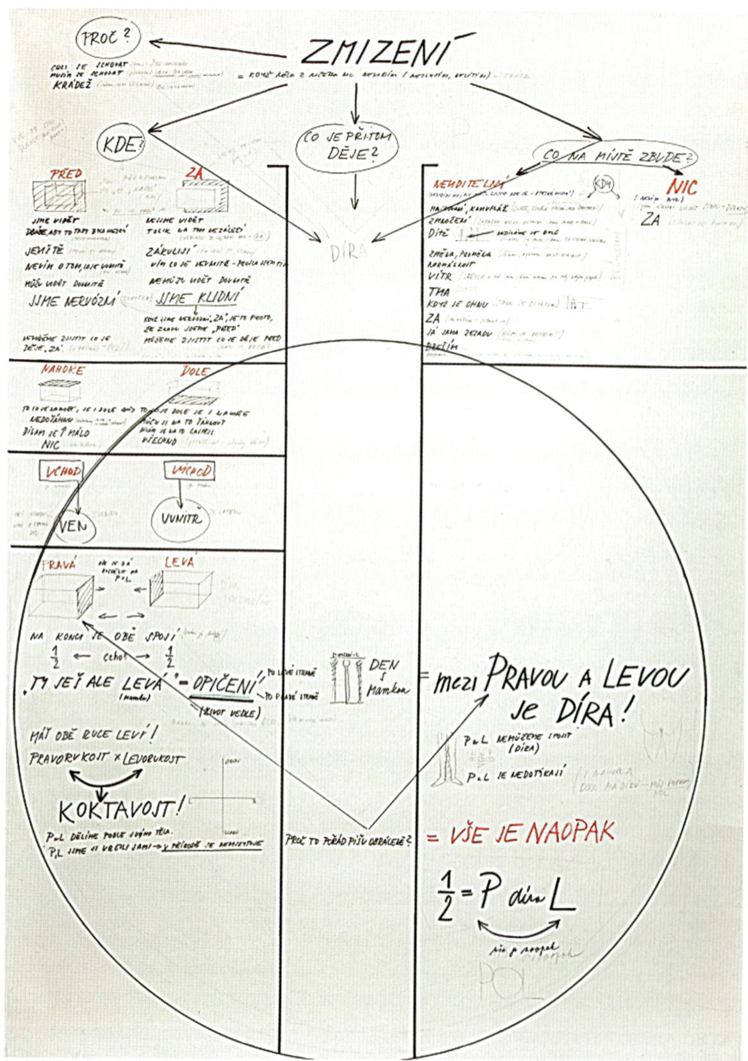

ILLUSTRATION 5.11 Kateřina Šedá, *Raising Children Basic Graph 3*, ink on paper, 2004. Courtesy of the artist.

Performing drawing

Related to this emerging tradition of collaborative drawing are drawing activities that encompass and divert ideas and methods from traditions of performance. For example, performance-derived ideas such as the 'stage' or arena for performance, call and response, focused and diffuse attention, and the use of the weight of the body are being translated into methods of thinking and making drawings. Robert Luzar (b.1980) uses these techniques, among others, to create drawings that challenge the objectification and commoditization of drawings as objects. Methods of performing drawing displace the drafter's body. Instead of the drafter's body being a focus for the branding of the drawing as an object, it vanishes and its traces become ineffable (see Illustration 3.10).

Moving drawings

Although Luzar's work appears to focus upon the individual drafter, as a performer of a drawing, in fact, the ensemble culture that underpins traditions of performance is very much in evidence. Performances are encounters between performers and audience. Luzar focuses his own and viewers' experiences of drawing by thinking of his drawing activities as taking place in a performance arena and directing an audience's attention. Drawings made for Japanese animation, called 'anime', make extensive use of these performance techniques, first, to streamline production but, ultimately, to create a specific sense of times and places for viewers.

In anime, there is an important distinction between 'drawing movement' and 'moving drawings'. The former refers to full animation, in which individual drawings disappear, to be replaced by the illusion of a fully mobile story world. In the latter, however, still drawings are themselves moved, in relation to a camera. This technique focuses attention on the physical mechanics of the production of both movement and the illusion of movement, implying a series of drafters' bodies, themselves moving within an arena establishing calls and responses between still and moving scenes and the audience.

Contemporary drawing and public cultural institutions

Contemporary drawing has not been the topic of major museum exhibitions in the West until relatively recently. The major exhibitions since the 1960s can be counted on one hand. The Museum of Modern Art in New York only established a Department of Drawing in 1971, using the 1976 exhibition *Drawing Now: 1955–1975*, to start to showcase the ways in which contemporary drafters were making and thinking about drawing. The exhibition explored the ways in which drawing had emerged fully fledged into the art world as a primary medium after the Second World War, offering drafters ways of bridging older divisions between 'abstraction' and 'figuration' (or what is now called depiction), between different media and between ideas about systems, notation and the drafter's body. In 1992, another survey exhibition at the Museum of Modern Art sought to consolidate the status of drawing. Titled *Allegories of Modernism: Contemporary Drawing*, it proposed that drawing can be thought of as a pervasive group of ideas that connects widely different cultures and, as a result, has been influential in many different disciplines and for many different purposes.

Since then, the Museum of Modern Art has committed itself to regular survey exhibitions, every ten years or so, that seek to make sense of the condition of contemporary drawing as a fine art. *Drawing Now: Eight Propositions* (2002) brought together multiple approaches to drawing, in the sciences and psychology, the decorative arts and storytelling, describing links between these different approaches. *On Line: Drawing Through the Twentieth Century* (2011) attempted to establish retrospectively the dominant trends in thinking about and making drawings with the benefit of the hindsight provided by the museum's preceding survey exhibitions.

Similar major survey exhibitions have focused upon other particular ideas about drawing. *The Primacy of Drawing* at the Hayward Gallery, London, in 1995, established a benchmark for ways of explaining every aspect of drawing, guided by numerous examples taken from the great collections of historic drawings housed in London's cultural institutions. In 2004, the exhibition *The Stage of Drawing: Gesture and Act* at the Tate Gallery, London, and the Drawing Centre, New York, went far beyond the established idea that the drafter's body is significant for drawing, considering in detail the relationships between mark making and ideas about performance.

Tracing the Century: Drawing as a Catalyst for Change, an exhibition at Tate Liverpool in 2012, brought together drawings made over the last one hundred years, to show how drawing has been used at the cutting edge of changes to societies and cultures, identities and technology. *Pushing Paper: Contemporary Drawing from 1970 to Now*, an exhibition at the British Museum, London, in 2020, sought again to provide the type of broad survey undertaken by the Museum of Modern Art's exhibition from the 1970s onwards.

These exhibitions have guided the emergence of a number of institutions, founded since the 1970s, which make contemporary drawing into a specialism. The most famous of these is the Drawing Centre in New York, founded in 1977, which aims to present, promote and disseminate the widest range of drawing activities and ideas about drawing. More recent institutions, such as the Drawing Room, founded in 2002, the Centre for Recent Drawing, founded in 2004 (both in London), and the Drawing Lab in Paris, founded in 2007, share this mission.

Although the widest variety of types of drawing are currently thriving and diversifying, in many circumstances, the opening of these institutions responded to the fact that drawing has not really been taught in higher education in the West since the 1950s. Artists who trained in the art school system in the United Kingdom since then, for example, found their training to be very different to their pre-war predecessors. With the revolution brought about by 'abstraction', in particular Abstract Expressionism, the craft skills associated with learning to draw, through observation, for example, were largely abandoned. At the same time, the continual search for novel varieties of fine art largely overturned the high status of historic fine art drawings. The new drawing institutions, such as the Drawing Centre, successfully sought to provide a source of information and experiences of drawing, continuity, ideas, participation and even training in drawing, in the face of this dearth.

Much more recently, a small number of public institutions have emerged that aim to support and celebrate particular types of drawing. Often these institutions have pioneered types of drawing (and types of drafter) that have long been sidelined, overlooked or ignored by mainstream institutions, such as comics or graffiti. These institutions find themselves in the unique position of being able to make explicit connections between contemporary drawing and the history of the types of drawing they focus upon, taking an even-handed view of a broader visual culture than museums and galleries that focus either on contemporary drawing or on historic drawing alone.

These institutions include the Centre Belge de la bande desinée (Belgian Centre for Comics) in Brussels, founded in 1982, La cité internationale de la bande desinée et de l'image (the International City of Comics and Images) in Angoulême, France, founded in 2008, and the Museum of Graffiti in Miami, founded in 2019. Very recently, this approach – bringing the history of drawing into the present day – has inspired some radical overhauls of historical drawing collections according to contemporary ideas. For example, the Sumida Hokusai Museum in Tokyo, founded in 2016, dedicated to understanding and promoting the drawings of the Japanese artist Hokusai (1760–1849), offers a radical reconsideration of the historic purposes and achievements of 'ukiyo-e' drawing (or 'pictures of a floating world') in the famous late Edo Period (1603–1868), according to insights gained from contemporary drafters.

SELECTIVE GLOSSARY

Aesthetic Aesthetic is borrowed from 'aesthesis', the Greek for 'sensation'. Aesthetic literally means 'sensational', which has a slightly different, though related, English meaning ('exciting').

Analogue Analogue media directly reproduces and rearranges properties that it shares with the objects it represents. This direct reproduction and rearrangement is described as analogous. For example, the colour of an analogue mark might be the same as the colour of the object it represents. A yellow mark might indicate a banana or a shaft of yellow sunlight because all of these things share the property 'yellow'.

Axonometric A drawing system in which parallel lines existing in the real world are always drawn as parallel, regardless of their perceived relative depth or their distance from the viewer. Axonometric systems often (but not always) rely upon the convention that, relative to each other, marks appearing lower in a drawing represent items that are nearer to the viewer than higher marks.

Colour Colour is the wavelength of light reflected from objects, resulting in perceived and imagined associations between these wavelengths and other material properties. Although these wavelengths are themselves properties, they are always perceived according to different biological capacities in different creatures, including humans.

Craft Craft is a body of knowledge producing learned capacities (skills) within particular circumstances. Although craft is associated with manual skills, manual manipulation and making (such as drawing, playing a musical instrument, writing or blacksmithing), techniques for gaining and making use of manual knowledge are now also applied to any learned capacities, such as game playing, mental arithmetic or theorization.

Depiction Depiction is a type of visual representation defined by both seeing the materials with which the depiction is made whilst simultaneously imagining that we see the object of the depiction. In depictions, the dual experience of vision (seeing marks) and visualization ('seeing-in' the object of depiction) is unlike any other experience of visual representation. In everyday language, the word 'figurative' is often substituted for 'depictive'.

Digital Digital is a method of generating representations by re-coding the things that are represented as series of two numerical values, 'zero' or 'one'. This code accumulates in different sequences to create commands. It is these commands that generate representations in different media.

Drafter A drafter makes drawings.

Feeling Feeling is often thought of as spontaneous emotion and sensation. However, feeling also encompasses some types of judgement that are not simply accompanied by spontaneously occurring emotions or sensations. These include ethical judgements of right and wrong, about which is commonly said 'I don't feel right about' a situation or 'it feels wrong'.

Force Dynamics Force dynamics are measures and types of energy, generated by making comparisons with other forces, as environmental features. For example, mass, size and motion are categories of time and space that are often thought of as resources that every body makes use of (how fast, strong, large or old a body is). When a force is applied, mass is a property of comparative resistance to changes in motion. Motion is a change in location in comparison to a frame of reference. Size is abstracted from comparative judgements of magnitude.

Index In drawing, a mark is always an indexical sign of the activity of its production. It signifies, in part, by indicating a physical connection with its object.

Line First, line is an abstract idea, representing two dimensions, extending the idea of a one-dimensional point. Neither point nor line has any material manifestation. They are ideas. A point is the idea of a location in space and a line is the idea of either an accumulation of adjacent points or the distance between two remote points. Second, however, line is also a trace of the direction in which a drafter forces the drawing medium, the material making a mark.

Local Tone, Local Colour The word local is used to describe a tone or colour that is inherent to an object, as opposed to a tone or colour created by atmospheric effects upon objects. An apple might be inherently red (its local colour), whilst appearing pink in early morning light or dark purple at night.

Mark A mark is any visual item that reproduces and represents the functional aspects of the system of representation from which it gains its meaning. These systems of representation include writing, mapping, any spatial projection, depictions and, ultimately, the conditions of the situation in which a mark is made and seen. In the sense that mark making defines drawing, the drawn mark cannot be identified outside a system of representation because it is the system that gives a mark meaning. This is what distinguishes drawn marks from any other random mark that we might see. No specific technology or set of social circumstances ever defines the mark.

Medium A medium is a set of agreed circumstances in which information is stored and transmitted. These agreed circumstances are often tied to specific forms of representation, which are themselves often tied to specific materials and social situations. For example, the medium of writing produces all of the wide range of circumstances in which writing is used, whilst the drawing medium produces all of the wide range of circumstances in which drawing is used. The circumstances in which a medium is used and the forms it adopts can be extremely various.

Mimesis The visual imitation of the visible world.

Monocular Literally, 'one-eyed'. Human vision is binocular, that is, produced by two eyes. Monocular vision establishes clues for the recognition of depth that have historically favoured the use of spatial projection systems to make two-dimensional representations of three-dimensional objects, offering and representing a single point of view.

Object An object is something observed. This definition relies upon the idea that human consciousness is subjective, that the world is not simply experienced when it is observed but, rather, the world is produced by observation. The human subject observes and the object is the thing (or the world) observed.

Objective (adjective) A description of a set of circumstances made without the use of judgement. An objective description aims to establish impartiality, or an absence of judgement, by identifying properties or characteristics that are self-evidencing. As such, objectivity (the capacity to make objective descriptions) is often associated with quantification and measurement, as distinct from emotion or sensation.

Properties Properties are experiences attributed to things. For example, the property 'red' might be attributed to an apple. Redness is not definitive of all apples, so redness exemplifies a particular (red) apple, without permanently modifying our expectations of apples in general. Words often substituted for 'properties' include 'features', 'characteristics' or 'qualities'.

Sign A sign is a representation or any entity that indicates the presence of something else. Within this broad definition, the tradition of semiotics (thinking about and explaining signs) identifies three ways in which signs function to represent other things: first, by making a physical connection between the sign and what it signifies; second, by having the sign resemble what it signifies; and, third, by using a learned set of conventions that dictate that the sign means something, that it is agreed that 'this' means 'that'.

Spatial Projection System A spatial projection system is a closed system of visual representation in which the location of marks on a two-dimensional surface systematically corresponds to the relative proximities between three-dimensional coordinates found in the viewed scene that is being represented. Spatial projection systems always create a systematic equivalence of the location of two-dimensional marks and three-dimensional coordinates.

Story Story encompasses everything that is told or shown, as structurally and functionally distinct from the activities of telling or showing. This definition allows the widest range of representations to be considered as stories, in every medium. It contradicts older definitions, which insist that stories can only be told in verbal media.

Style Style is the specific degrees to which the manufacture of an individual representation or object resembles or differs from the manufacture of other manufactured representations or objects.

Subject The subject is a human observer of the world. This definition relies upon the idea that human consciousness is subjective, that the world is not simply experienced when it is observed but, rather, the world is produced by observation. The human subject observes and the object is the thing (or the world) observed.

Subjective A description of a set of circumstances made using judgement. A subjective description establishes a partial view based on the human subject's emotions and ideas. As such, subjectivity (the capacity to make judgements) produces the identity of the subject or produces the relationships between the subject and the world rather than describing observations of the world.

Symbol A symbol is a type of sign that makes use of a learned set of conventions. These conventions dictate that the sign means something, that it is agreed that 'this' means 'that'. Symbols differ from two other types of sign, indexical signs, which make a physical connection between the sign and what it signifies, and iconic signs, which resemble what they signify.

Technology Technology is any item or situation that modifies, transforms or produces capacities of the human body.

Tone Tone is a relative degree of the presence of light (lightness or darkness), measured by comparison with other degrees of light.

Trace Traces are the direct remnants of drawing activities. Traces index, or point to, the activity of the body from which they originate, but they also leave remnants. Trace is a subset of index.

Type Type is the identification of a subject, object or situation by applying knowledge of shared properties to specific instances. These properties are understood to be held in common, so that any subject, object or situation displaying these properties is also understood as belonging to the same type.

Visualization Visualization is visual imagining, a type of mental representation. Whilst not necessarily related to experiences of the world outside the body, such as vision, visualizations are themselves perceived. As such, visualizations conform in structure and function to perceptions, even if they are not related to any other perceived experience.

BIBLIOGRAPHY

Introduction

Billen, Andrew, 'I don't know much about children. I just draw them', *The Times Weekend* (30 May 2020), p. 9.

Chapter 1: Imitation

Adams, Eileen, 'Power Drawing: Campaign for Drawing', *Engage*, no. 10 (2001), pp. 2–10.

Berger, John and Jim Savage, *Berger on Drawing* (Aghabullogue, Ireland: Occasional Press, 1996).

Cramer, Charles A., 'Alexander Cozens's "New Method": The Blot and General Nature-Painter', *Art Bulletin*, 79, no. 1 (1997), pp. 112–129.

de Zegher, Catherine, *The Stage of Drawing: Gesture and Act* (London: Tate Publishing, 2003).

Freedman, Luba, *Titian's Portraits Through Aretino's Lens* (University Park: Pennsylvania State University Press, 1995).

Plato, *Republic*, Book III (Oxford: Oxford University Press, 2008), 3.392c–398b.

Ruskin, John, *The Elements of Drawing* (London: A & C Black, 2007).

Taussig, Michael, *Mimesis and Alterity: A Particular History of the Senses* (London: Routledge, 1993).

Wollheim, Richard, *Art and Its Objects* (Cambridge: Cambridge University Press, 1980).

Wollheim, Richard, *Painting as an Art* (Princeton, NJ: Princeton University Press, 1987).

Chapter 2: Mark

Andersen, Kirsty, *The Geometry of an Art: The History of the Mathematical Theory of Perspective from Alberti to Monge* (New York: Springer, 2007).

Billeter, J. F., *The Chinese Art of Writing* (New York: Rizzoli International, 1990).

Gardner, Jared, 'Storylines', *Substance*, 40, no. 124 (2011), pp. 53–69.

Geismar, Haidy, 'Drawing It Out', *Visual Anthropology Review*, no. 30 (2014), pp. 97–113.

Goodman, Nelson, *Languages of Art: An Approach to a Theory of Symbols* (Indianapolis, IN: Bobbs-Merrill, 1969).

Grennan, Simon, *A Theory of Narrative Drawing* (New York: Palgrave Macmillan, 2017).

Guynes, Sean, 'Four-Color Sound: A Peircean Semiotics of Comic Book Onomatopoeia', *Public Journal of Semiotics*, 6, no. 1 (2014), pp. 58–72.

Halliday, Michael, *Spoken and Written Language* (Geelong, Victoria: Deakin University Press, 1985).

Harris, Roy, *Rethinking Writing* (New York: Continuum, 2002).

Hendrickson, Carol, 'Visual Field Notes: Drawing Insights in the Yucatan', *Visual Anthropology Review*, no. 24 (2008), pp. 117–132.

Ingold, Tim, *Lines: A Brief History* (London: Routledge, 2007).

Jarombek, Mark, 'The Structural Problematic of Leon Battista Alberti's De pictura', *Renaissance Studies*, 4, no. 3 (1990), pp. 273–285.

Klee, Paul, *Paul Klee: The Thinking Eye* (London: Lund Humphries, 1964).

Martin, J. R., *English Text: System and Structure* (Philadelphia, PA: John Benjamins, 1992).

Maynard, Patrick, *Drawing Distinctions* (Ithaca, NY: Cornell University Press, 2005).

McIver Lopes, Dominic, 'Drawing in a Social Science: Lithic Illustration', *Perspectives on Science*, 17, no. 1 (2009), pp. 5–25.

Powell, Barry, *Writing: Theory and History of the Technology of Civilisation* (London: Wiley-Blackwell, 2009).

Rawson, Philip, *Seeing Through Drawing* (London: BBC Books, 1979).

Rawson, Philip, *Drawing* (University Park: University of Pennsylvania Press, 1987).

Rendgen, Sandra, *The Minard System: The Graphical Works of Charles-Joseph Minard* (New York: Princeton Architectural Press, 2018).

Rosand, David, *Drawing Acts: Studies in Graphic Expression and Representation* (New York: Cambridge University Press, 2002).

Thibault, Paul, *Brain, Mind and the Signifying Body: An Ecosocial Semiotic Theory* (London: Continuum, 2004).

Thomas, Nigel, 'Are Theories of Imagery Theories of Imagination? An Active Perception Approach to Conscious Mental Content', *Cognitive Science*, no. 23 (1999), pp. 207–245.

Willats, Stephen, *Art and Representation: New Principles in the Analysis of Pictures* (Princeton, NJ: Princeton University Press, 1997).

Woodward, David and Malcolm Lewis, *The History of Cartography, Volume 2, Book 3: Cartography in the Traditional African, American, Arctic, Australian and Pacific Societies* (Chicago: University of Chicago Press, 1998).

Yen, Y., *Calligraphy and Power in Contemporary Chinese Society* (London: Routledge, 2005).

Chapter 3: Trace

Bergson, Henri, *Creative Evolution* (New York: Dover Publications, 2007).

Butler Williams, C. E., *A Manual for Teaching Model-Drawing from Solid Forms, the Models Founded on Those of M. Dupuis* (London: J. W. Parker, 1843), pp. 237–251.

de Beauvoir, Simone, *The Second Sex* (Harmondsworth, UK: Penguin, 1953).

Descartes, René, *The Philosophical Writings of Descartes* (Cambridge: Cambridge University Press, 1988).

Douglas, Jack, *Understanding Everyday Life: Toward the Reconstruction of Sociological Knowledge* (London: Routledge & Kegan Paul, 1974).

Dworkin, Andrea, *Women Hating: A Radical Look at Sexuality* (New York: Dutton, 1974).

Fanon, Franz, *Black Skin, White Masks* (London: Pluto Press, 1986).

Gardner, Jared, 'Storylines', *Substance*, 40, no.124 (2011), pp. 53–69.

Grennan, Simon, *A Theory of Narrative Drawing* (New York: Palgrave Macmillan, 2017).

Hosea, Birgitta, 'Drawing Animation', *Animation*, no. 5 (2010), pp. 353–367.

Husserl, Edmund, *Cartesian Meditations: An Introduction to Phenomenology* (The Hague: Martinus Nijhoff, 2013).

Krauss Rosalind, *The Originality of the Avant-Garde and Other Modernist Myths* (Cambridge, MA: MIT Press, 1985).

McClintock, Anne, *Imperial Leather: Race, Gender and Sexuality in the Colonial Context* (London: Routledge, 1995).

Merleau-Ponty, Maurice, *The Phenomenology of Perception* (London: Routledge, 1978).

Munro, T., 'Style in the Arts: A Method of Stylistic Analysis', *Journal of Aesthetics and Art Criticism*, 5, no. 2 (1946), pp. 128–158.

Munsterberg, Marjorie, *Writing about Art* (Seattle: Create Space Independent Publishing, 2009), pp. 21–27.

Newton, Esther, *Mother Camp: Female Impersonators in America* (Chicago: University of Chicago Press, 1972).

Pierce, Charles, *The Essential Pierce: Selected Philosophical Writings, Volume 2: 1893–1913* (Bloomington: Indiana University Press, 1998).

Rosand, David, *Drawing Acts: Studies in Graphic Expression and Representation* (New York: Cambridge University Press, 2002).

Schütz, Alfred, *The Phenomenology of the Social World* (Evanston, IL: Northwestern University Press, 1972).

Siddons, Henry, *Practical Illustrations of Rhetorical Gesture and Action: Adapted to the English Drama* (London: Richard Phillips, 1807).
Smolderen, Thierry, *The Origin of Comics* (Jackson: University Press of Mississippi, 2014).

Chapter 4: Story

Baetens, Jan, 'Revealing Traces: A New Theory of Graphic Enunciation', in Robin Varnum and Christina Gibbons (eds), *The Language of Comics: Word and Image*, pp. 145–155 (Jackson: University Press of Mississippi, 2001).
Benveniste, Émile, *Problems in General Linguistics* (Coral Gables, FL: University of Miami Press, 1971).
Chatman, Seymour, *Story and Discourse: Narrative Structure in Fiction and Film* (Ithaca, NY: Cornell University Press, 1978).
Gaudreault, André, *From Plato to Lumière: Narration and Monstration in Literature and Cinema* (Toronto: University of Toronto Press, 2009).
Goodman, Nelson, *Languages of Art: An Approach to a Theory of Symbols* (Indianapolis, IN: Bobbs-Merrill, 1969).
Kukkonen, Karin, *Studying Comics and Graphic Novels* (Hoboken, NJ: Wiley, 2013).
Lessing, Gottfried, *Laocoon: An Essay upon the Limits of Painting and Poetry, with Remarks Illustrative of Various Points in the History of Ancient Art* (Boston, MA: Little, Brown, 1904).
Marion, Philippe, *Traces en cass: Travail graphique, figuration narrative et participation du lecteur* (Louvain-la-neuve: Université Catholique de Louvain, 1993).
Mikkonen, Kai, *The Narratology of Comic Art* (New York: Routledge, 2017).
Plato, *Republic*, Book III (Oxford: Oxford University Press, 2008), 3.392c–398b.
Ruskin, John, *The Elements of Drawing* (London: A & C Black, 2007).
Shklovsky, Viktor, 'Art as Technique', in L. T. Lemon and J. R. Reis (eds), *Russian Formalist Criticism*, pp. 3–24 (Lincoln: University of Nebraska Press, 2012).
Weinrich, Harald, *Tempus - Besprochene und erzählte Welt* (Stuttgart: Kohlhammer, 1964).

Chapter 5: Drawing today

Abbate, Carolyn, *Unsung Voices: Opera and Musical Narrative in the Nineteenth Century* (Princeton, NJ: Princeton University Press, 1996).
Butler, Cornelia and Catherine de Zegher, *On Line: Drawing Through the Twentieth Century* (New York: Museum of Modern Art, 2011).

Darwin, Charles, *The Expression of the Emotions in Man and Animals* (New York: Oxford University Press, 2009).

de Zegher, Catherine, *The Stage of Drawing: Gesture and Act* (London: Tate Publishing, 2003).

Hoptman, Laura J., *Drawing Now: Eight Propositions* (New York: Museum of Modern Art, 2002).

Ingold, Tim, *Being Alive: Essays on Movement, Knowledge and Description* (New York: Routledge, 2011).

Katz, Jack, *How Emotions Work* (Chicago: University of Chicago Press, 1991).

McNeill, David, *Hand and Mind: What Gestures Reveal about Thought* (Chicago, IL: University of Chicago Press, 1992).

Nancy, Jean-Luc, *The Pleasure in Drawing* (New York: Fordham University Press, 2013).

Petherbridge, Deanna, *The Primacy of Drawing: Histories and Theories of Practice* (London: Yale University Press, 2010).

Rose, Bernice, *Drawing Now: 1955–1975* (New York: Museum of Modern Art, 1976).

Rose, Bernice, *Allegories of Modernism: Contemporary Drawing* (New York: Museum of Modern Art, 1992).

Tormey, Jane, Andrew Selby, Phil Sawdon, Russell Marshall and Simon Downs, *Drawing Now: Between the Line of Contemporary Art* (London: I.B.Tauris, 2007).

FURTHER READING

Allen, Laura and Luke Caspar Pearson (eds), *Drawing Futures* (London: Riverside Architectural, 2016).

Anderson, Gemma, *Drawing as a Way of Knowing in Art and Science* (London: Intellect, 2017).

Berger, John and Jim Savage, *Berger on Drawing* (Aghabullogue, Ireland: Occasional Press, 1996).

Bryson, Norman, *Visual Theory: Painting and Interpretation* (New York: HarperCollins, 1989).

Butler, Cornelia, *Afterimage: Draw Through Process* (Boston, MA: MIT Press, 1999).

Camhy, Sherry, *Art of the Pencil: Revolutionary Look at Drawing, Painting and the Pencil* (New York: Watson-Guptil, 1997).

Campbell, Andy, *Queer X Design: 50 Years of Signs, Symbols, Banners, Logos and Graphic Art* (London: Black Dog & Leventhal, 2019).

Casey, Sarah and Gerry Davies, *Drawing Investigations* (London: Bloomsbury Visual Arts, 2020).

Chaet, Bernard, *The Art of Drawing* (New York: Holt, Rinehart and Winston, 1970).

Chorpening, Kelly and Rebecca Fortnum (eds.), *A Companion to Contemporary Drawing* (Hoboken: Wiley Blackwell, 2021).

de Zegher, Catherine, *The Stage of Drawing: Gesture and Act* (London: Tate Publishing, 2003).

Farthing, Stephen, *Dirtying the Paper Delicately* (London: University of the Arts, 2005).

Foa, Maryclare, Jane Grisewood, Birgitta Hosea and Carali McCall, *Performance Drawing: New Practices since 1945* (London: Bloomsbury Visual Arts, 2020).

Goldstein, Nathan, *The Art of Responsive Drawing* (London: Pearson, 2005).

Grennan, Simon, *A Theory of Narrative Drawing* (New York: Palgrave Macmillan (2017).

Hoptman, Laura J., *Drawing Now: Eight Propositions* (New York: Museum of Modern Art, 2002).

Kantor, Jordan, Igor Zabel and Emma Dexter, *Vitamin D: New Perspectives in Drawing* (New York: Phaidon Press, 2005).

Leymarie, Jean, Genevieve Monnier and Bernice Rose, *Drawing: History of an Art* (London: Macmillan, 1979).

Marshall, Russell and Phil Sawdon, *Hyperdrawing: Beyond the Line of Contemporary Art* (London: I.B.Tauris, 2012).

Marshall, Russell and Phil Sawdon, *Drawing Ambiguity: Beside the Lines of Contemporary Art* (London: I.B.Tauris, 2015).

Maynard, Patrick, *Drawing Distinctions* (Ithaca, NY: Cornell University Press, 2005).

Mendelowitz, Daniel M., *A Guide to Drawing* (Boston, MA: Cengage Learning, 1980).

Meskimmon, Marsha and Phil Sawdon, *Drawing Difference* (London: Bloomsbury Visual Arts, 2016).

Nancy, Jean-Luc, *The Pleasure of Drawing* (New York: Fordham University Press, 2013).

Perry, Colin, Marina Cashdan and Carina Krause, *Vitamin D2: New Perspectives in Drawing* (New York: Phaidon Press, 2013).

Petherbridge, Deanna, *The Primacy of Drawing: Histories and Theories of Practice* (London: Yale University Press, 2010).

Powel, Richard J., *Black Art: A Cultural History* (London: Thames and Hudson, 2002).

Rawson, Philip, *Seeing Through Drawing* (London: BBC Books, 1979).

Rawson, Philip, *Drawing* (University Park, PA: University of Pennsylvania Press, 1987).

Reilly, Maura, *Women Artists: The Linda Nochlin Reader* (New York: Thames & Hudson, 2015).

Rosand, David, *Drawing Acts: Studies in Graphic Expression and Representation* (New York: Cambridge University Press, 2002).

Schenk, Pamela, *Drawing in the Design Process* (Bristol: Intellect, 2016).

Speed, Harold, *The Practice and Science of Drawing* (New York: Dover Publications, 2003).

Stout, Katherine, *Contemporary Drawing: From the 1960s to Now* (London: Tate Publishing, 2014).

Tormey, Jane, Andrew Selby, Phil Sawdon, Russell Marshall and Simon Downs, *Drawing Now: Between the Line of Contemporary Art* (London: I.B.Tauris, 2007).

Willats, Stephen, *Art and Representation: New Principles in the Analysis of Pictures* (Princeton, NJ: Princeton University Press, 1997).

INDEX